FINDING
BISHOP CASTLE

A Road Trip to Recovery

by Jeff Bowersox

FINDING BISHOP CASTLE

First Edition: November 2021

Edited by Elizabeth Jahns

ISBN: 978-0-578-88261-1

For those who no longer want to settle and compromise,

but desire a profound *better*…

CONTENTS

Prologue

Tammy and I had nestled ourselves into a small nook at The Speedtrap Bistro. For a tiny coffee shop that served light French fare, it was unusually busy for the late evening hour. Our intent was to find a quiet spot to debrief, scroll through the photos we had gathered, and recount the day. A day that had started with zero expectations, unfolding into adventure and insights beyond what we could have foreseen for a lazy Saturday. A ridiculous, spontaneous day.

The reason for the hum and bustle of the café became clear as our server offered to put in our drink orders. The Speedtrap was no longer just our mid-morning coffee spot; late Saturday, it was a bar.

Tammy made eye contact with me first to silently ask if it was okay to order a drink, and then redirected to the server after my approving nod. "I'll have a vodka and cranberry."

The server looked at me. "And for you? Beer, cocktail, glass of wine?"

"Oh, no… No thank you. I don't drink. I'll have a double-shot Americano, black. Stronger than you think is reasonable."

Feeling the buzz of my phone, I slid it out of my pocket to check the screen. "I'm going to step outside really quick. It's Nathan."

Nathan had recently sprung into his first semester of college. While Tammy and I were enjoying an early bout of empty nesting, we took his phone calls, almost nightly, with eager anticipation.

"Hey, Dad. How was your day? What'd you guys do?"

Not knowing where to start or how to fit the day's events into a small conversation befitting an outdoor bar patio, I began with what must have sounded like a shotgun blast of gibberish. "Our day was so incredible, it's hard to explain. There's a place I always wanted to take you as a kid, a far off castle in the middle of the mountains. I don't remember if I ever brought it up. I wasn't even sure it was real. There's this castle, built by a single man over his lifetime. He's been doing it for over 50 years. We just decided to go there today on a whim. It sounds so implausible, but it was really there! We got to meet the guy who built it, and he was all of about five-foot-four, if that. He's maybe 75 years old now. He just sat there, watching people tour his castle, sometimes yelling. It was so inspiring, Nathan. I mean, my face and the back of my head hurt in the creases. They hurt from smiling. Seriously, I think I've been grinning all day long!"

Nathan sensed an exuberance in me that he wasn't expecting. Responding with a half-fake laugh, he said, "*Okay*. Let's see... So, you went to the mountains in the middle of nowhere to see a castle that a small, yelling, elderly man built all by himself? Are you sure you didn't just join a cult?"

I laughed, but also hesitated while second-guessing my fervent delivery. "No... Uh, we..."

I heard him move his mouth away from the phone and then shout to his dorm mates over his shoulder teasingly, "Hey everyone, I think my dad just joined a cult!"

Chapter 1

The Bedroom

<u>10:15 AM</u>

My first awareness of consciousness blended with the auditory sound of a gurgle, liquid fizzling. Creeping through our bedroom window was the pleasant sound of the sprinkler head collapsing. A crisp morning breeze traveled along with the satisfaction of a chore being completed while I had slept. Our lawn already watered, I took in the morning air, rolling over to fix my eyes on Tammy. I lapped my arm across her abdomen, sinking into the plush down comforter.

Already sitting up, enjoying her coffee, Tammy said, "Boise is out."

"Huh?" I was silently resentful that she was already so clearly caffeinated.

"Boise's out. We can't move to Boise and be a part of the next hippest city if it's already being listed in the top ten best places to live." She thrust her phone in my face.

I sighed and contemplated playing along with her banter.

Tammy and I grew up in the suburbs of Denver and have seen explosive growth in our city over the last 20 years. We often played a game of escapism, trying to determine where the next bang for our real estate dollar could land us. We always thought Portland and Austin were "cool" before they were cool, and lately Boise, Idaho had been our most recent location for imaginary prospecting.

"That's it," she said. "I think we should just create our own hipster town. We'll buy an old barren industrial city in Kentucky and invite the most famous people in every trade. Maybe we can have The Discovery Channel film it, like a reality series or something."

I rolled out of bed to head for the kitchen. As I returned and set my coffee on the nightstand, she continued, "I think it could work. Like, how Chip and Joanna made Waco cool. Who could we invite? Do we know any famous people?"

I took a sip. "I think we should have Jack White curate the arts. Like, have a theater and maybe a record store."

"Not a bad start." Tammy smiled. "What about education? Fashion? Architecture?"

"Jack White. I think we can have him do that stuff, too."

"And restaurants? What famous chefs would you invite?"

Sadly, my initial promptings were of creators like Anthony Bourdain, Kate Spade, and Hunter S. Thompson, icons who had let alcohol play a role in taking their talents from us too soon.

I rolled back over and put my arm around Tammy, tickling her side in frustration. "You're making me think too much for a Saturday. I don't know, I mean, Jack's in six bands, has his own label... He's an author, actor, and a board member of the Library of Congress. Shit, I think he makes his own furniture. Don't you think he can do the cooking, too?"

"Well, maybe we should make him Mayor, then?"

"Hey now," I retorted. "I think I'd like to be considered first for Mayor?"

"I'm not voting for you," she teased. "You can't even get us a real chef."

Somehow, we rabbit-trailed into me sounding like an overbearing dictator levying fines to residents who wore skinny jeans or scarfs when the temperature climbed above 70 degrees. After some laughter, we decided I was too judgmental to govern my own town.

I'd say it started out like any other Saturday, but that wouldn't be true. *We had nothing to do.* There wasn't a volleyball match lined up or a workout class to attend, and the cool fall weather slowed the growth of our yard, begging us to skip chores for one weekend.

The recognition of a schedule void was both welcomed and intriguing.

Clarity and awareness return quickly on a Saturday morning. I can't say that was always the case in our relationship—or for most of it, really—but I am sober now.

◻˝F ฿ €˝◻

In times past, Saturday mornings were always preceded by Friday nights full of drunken monologues and alcohol-fueled ideas for the weekend ahead. Once the week's work crises and political scandals had been resolved, Tammy and I would begin discussing all that we would accomplish. Increasingly, in tainted speech, we would plan a hike on the South Platte River, just a few miles away. Facebook notifications for events would pop up on our phones, enticing us to make a token appearance at an acquaintance's birthday party. We conceived of heading to the farmer's market the next morning, gathering ingredients to cook an elaborate meal. We might even plan some charity work. As the consumption of liquor grew, so did our ambitions. We'd start planning what it would take to add a guest cottage to our mountain property, derailing us into the wee hours watching tiny house videos on YouTube.

Alcohol slid us into that sweet spot, warm, laughing. We passed the phone back and forth to watch our favorite music videos, thinking we were singing the lyrics with precision, not realizing that our brains were at least a half measure behind.

It's not easy to consider quitting drinking, ever, but certainly not in those moments. It is *why* you drink. Our work week had been released, the stress and strain of responsibilities wiped from our mental inbox; monotony turned into excitement. We had solidarity in our goofiness. Shit... we were allowed to just *be goofy*. We were in love, our kids were healthy, and our bills were paid. We deserved it.

To peek into the repetitive, yet seemingly justifiable, use of alcohol with Tammy would not trip any major alarms. However, because our relationship hadn't begun until I was 36 years old, I'd had massive, traumatic alcohol-related moments prior to ever meeting her. Those alarms would blister the toughest of senses:

I made that 3 AM phone call to my best friend, Jim, in drunken despair, sobbing at the revelation that my first wife of 16 years had been with someone else. I had my closest family members folding their arms in worry, standing over my hospital bed, surveying my broken bones. My wrists had been zip tied by the police in front of everyone in Nathan's charter school parking lot during carpool. Someone notified my friends on the day of their wedding that I – the officiant – wouldn't be there. What had started with one drink the night before the wedding, putting pen to paper to write their ceremony, spiraled into self-pity and a drunken anguish that not only led me to not believe in love, but, for a terrifying moment, not even believe in life.

And if those big "E"s on the eyechart didn't compel me to quit drinking before I met Tammy, I certainly ignored the decade's worth of soul-crushing fine print underneath: taking a day drink in the morning for the first time to calm my shaking hands, going out of my way to a different liquor store than the one I went to the night before, keeping a further talking distance from others to screen my breath, and building daily alcohol-induced anxiety that crippled me from completing the simplest of tasks.

But, somehow, I managed to navigate my worst drinking consequences and shake that Etch-a-Sketch of a life into a blank canvas. I got to hit the reset button. *I met Tammy*. She was a chance to wipe the slate clean and start over. I considered the causes of my past alcohol abuse and the penalties that accrued as being environmental. I had a former spouse that betrayed me, humiliated me. There were work-related changes that put me at home, bored. I was a parent, both Mom and Dad on most days.

Things would be different with Tammy. I was happy, fulfilled. I wasn't in emotional pain. We shared an intense love and equitable partnership, beyond what I had even considered possible in my previous years. With her, surely I'd be able to drink like a *normal person*...

Tammy and I had a lot planned on those weekends when we drank. We would begrudgingly stop the private Friday party in hopes of having a full weekend experience. Tammy could leave her drink half finished before getting ready for bed. Out of sight, I would finish it for her. I started to recognize hints of the same compulsions that had blanketed my worst drinking days, but as my mental benchmarks would assure me, I wasn't as bad as I used to be. I would pull one more drink from the bottle as I passed through the kitchen. If I drank enough before bed, I could sleep through the morning. If I didn't, I would wake up wanting more. I should be allowed to sleep... After all, it's the weekend.

Our cultivated plans were noble ideas greased by liquor-enhanced delusions, but often they crumbled under the weight of a Saturday hangover. If our plans were remembered at all, the sting of lethargy usually won the day, and maybe the next.

◻"F Ƀ €"◻

Not this Saturday. I'm in recovery, 21 months sober. I've disconnected alcohol enough from my routine that it doesn't plague my every moment, but I am not so far removed that waking up on a Saturday morning alive and anticipating the day still feels like a novel idea, and one that I am grateful for.

"What do you want to do today?" Tammy asked, picking up her coffee from the nightstand.

"I don't know," I said, stretching. "We should do something, right?"

"We can do anything we want. Anything!"

It's true. Anything. Without drinking the night prior, we were spry, revitalized, and not hindered by a night full of promises poisoned.

We batted around some new ideas. We thought of paddle boarding on our neighborhood lake. We had purchased a new home last year in an ideal Colorado suburb, but the summer gave way with us not using the surrounding area as much as we would have liked.

Sober, we were trying our hand at adulting a little more so than in the past. The demands of installing our landscaping and grounding ourselves at our jobs left less time for local recreation, but even now, walking over to the lake seemed less adventurous than what we had in mind. It would always be there.

I suggested we drive to Cripple Creek, a gold rush era location turned into a mountain gambling town.

"We don't gamble," Tammy said, softly rebutting my idea.

"I know." I rolled over and wrapped my arm around her. "But what if we just walked in with gray suits like Tom Cruise and Dustin Hoffman in *Rain Man* and place $20 on 17 at the roulette wheel and walk off whether it hits or not. We'd have a nice mountain drive and get a great story out of the deal."

Tammy, eyebrows furrowed, asked, "I think they played Blackjack? Do we know how to play Blackjack?"

"No. We don't gamble."

We continued to sip coffee in bed and scroll on our phones. Maybe we'd combine a fondue restaurant with an open mic night.

We looked at the productions our local theaters were putting on: "Rocky Horror Picture Show" or "Always…Patsy Cline." Nah… One we'd seen and the other seemed like forced eccentricity.

We weren't on a time schedule and had no concrete plans. Lying around for a while, I was beginning to question whether we were just daydreaming. It would be okay if we all we did was bury ourselves in sweatpants and order Chinese. In these busy times, we didn't get enough of that.

I don't know how it struck me. Maybe it was spurred on by considering the mountain drive earlier, but I remembered something I had wanted to do many times over the last 20 years: visit Bishop Castle. I remember the first time I had heard about it. I was a young, poor father in my twenties, typing in "FREE THINGS TO DO IN

SOUTHERN COLORADO" on 56K dial-up internet. I remember the intrigue I had in finding this place online. The very idea of it seemed weird and unreal. It was an inconvenient drive, two and a half hours away, in a desolate area that couldn't possibly live up to its internet description: a castle built by one man, Jim Bishop, by hand, over a period of 50-plus years. Who builds a castle in the middle of nowhere? Who builds a castle anywhere?

I had shelved the idea when I had first learned of it. Then, it was because that long of a drive in an unreliable Ford Escort station wagon was not a sure thing, neither in fuel expense nor in wanting to end up broken down and stranded.

Multiple times since, I had thought about the castle. Is it real? Was it an internet hoax, dooming me to disappointment? Would it be like impulsively pulling off a sideroad on a Kansas highway to see the world's largest ball of tinfoil, except you had to organize your whole day to get there? For many reasons, I never followed through with going to see for myself.

Given that phone surfing for an adventure seemed to be what this lazy morning was all about, I dusted the cobwebs off of this lingering idea. Without the same definitive ease of my first search, I muddled through all the ad pop-ups and paid Google sponsors trying to direct me to where I didn't want to go.

I found it. Bishop Castle.

As it had in years past, the rather crude website seemed to say that there was a spectacle to behold, but the lack of pragmatism in someone spending their life building a structure in the middle of nowhere left me skeptical. The risk was this: should the destination be a bust, in a remote place called Rye, Colorado, bordering the San Isabel National Forest, there wouldn't be any other options of things to do if we had to call an audible. But what's an adventure without risk?

I struck a slightly more serious tenor. "I think I have an idea…"

After I fumbled through an explanation of what might have been the most irrational thing to do with our time, Tammy asked, "Do you think it'll be safe?"

With the steeliest of Indiana Jones eyes I could muster, I said, "I hope not."

Taking her last sip, she whipped the comforter across my face and scooched out of bed. "I can be ready in 20 minutes."

I wasn't sure what getting sober would look like almost 21 months ago. Towards the end, it was never the shame of outward pressure or even the consequences that drove me to quit. Most certainly, I would never grant anyone or any circumstance the autonomy to tell me how to live.

If anything, what kept me from quitting earlier was the fear of missing out. In part, I was terrified to uncover whether Tammy's and my fun, love, and excitement was always due to being primed with drinks.

Was our joy and connectedness catalyzed by our affection and repetitive use of alcohol?

But that morning, I watched Tammy climb out of bed and studied her upbeat, bouncy stride as she passed by me. There we were, late-morning on a Saturday, still in love, still energetic and spontaneous, and apparently, because we were embarking on a real-life episode of Finding Bishop's Castle... *still goofy*.

Fear of missing out? We weren't missing a thing.

Chapter 2
The Driveway

11:20 AM

You settle into the vehicle. "Did you feed Shelby?"

You adjust the driver's seat. "Have you seen my eyedrops?"

The mirrors get adjusted. "Do we have a second USB cord?"

You turn the k… "Shit, sorry… I left my coffee in the microwave."

It didn't matter. We spoke easily and joyously. We approached the freedom of midday, where nothing is pressing and, if not said explicitly, our expectations were low. I nestled back into the driver's seat, placing the travel mug in the center console. Tammy reached for my forearm, giving it an excited shake.

It's not a thing, anyway. In no legendary journey in any story ever told does it start with, "and so he left the driveway." At best, it's a detail in the margins.

But not for me. The very act of getting in the car with the certainty of me driving it, or the car even starting at all, flushes me with gratitude. I paused, taking in a deep contemplative breath, grateful for my mobility.

◦"F Ƀ €"◦

I received my first drunk driving charge about 11 years ago. I consider it my "training wheels" DUI.

I had assembled an impressive existence thus far. Entering my early thirties with my first wife, Mindy, and our son, Nathan, we were comfortably settled into our third house. We climbed from the starter home, were buffered by the "not just right" home, and landed with our "forever home," coupled with neighbors where we felt we could be comfortable long-term. It had the space to grow, a cul-de-sac setting presenting picturesque safety, and neighbor relationships boasting vitality.

Mindy and I had started early. Married at age 18, we had a slight head start on our counterparts trying to land in the same pristine suburban community.

Shortly out of high school and newly married, I had obtained my first "adult" job at a biomedical and genetics research institute. I was a Core Laboratory

Technician, which was a really rich way of stating: Glorified Dishwasher. For an 18-year-old, approaching the four-story brick building in Denver, lined with hundred-year-old oak trees, prompted a slight tingle of inner importance. Leaving behind the poor optics of working fast food or retail, if I could learn to say my job title and tell people that I sterilized laboratory instruments, it had the potential to impress beyond any ambitions I thought of on my own. In the mornings, I would walk around the laboratories collecting glass flasks, beakers, and pipettes, measuring instruments that were nestled alongside fantastical machines. I'd study in wonder at the centrifuges and incubators, curious of their purpose. The crisp, neat atmosphere, intellectually prestigious, encased me in innovative importance.

I grew to love it. Fascinated by the microbiology lab next to my sterilizing room, an elderly technician created a variety of cell culture medias (artificial fluids that could mimic blood and grow the various cell culture lines that the researchers would study upstairs). I made it a point to get my work done as quickly and effectively as possible. This freed me to observe the lab next door, learn some basic chemistry and microbiology, and read what I later learned was the "go-to" textbook for colleges, *Molecular Biology of the Cell.*

Within a year and a half, the researchers upstairs felt that I could begin managing the microbiology in that lab. In my new position, I repeated the same cycle. I completed my work efficiently and with precision, and then began to learn cell culture and cytogenetics. Working in the Cytogenetics Lab next, it was rinse and repeat. Within four years, I had a full-time job as a Professional Research Assistant in one of the most prestigious laboratories in the state. We worked on Chromosome 21-related diseases (Down Syndrome, Alzheimer's, and ALS) and acted as the consortium that reconciled the sequencing of Chromosome 21 for The Human Genome Project.

I loved my work. I was good at it, and never did I misunderstand that a newly married, undereducated kid enjoyed a great privilege in participating in the sciences as an occupation. I observed early on the certain entitlements for the other researchers. Their four to ten years of undergraduate and postgraduate studies granted them staying power in their careers, and rightly so. But for me, I had to learn, produce data, and people please every day to earn my value.

As post-9/11 policies and the Bush presidency strained NIH grants, colleagues with a stronger pedigree than myself were dismissed, allowing me to stay through multiple rounds of job cuts. By the end of my tenure in the sciences, I had been an author in three scientific journals and was responsible for isolating clones and sequencing the missing gaps of human DNA on Chromosome 21, an achievement that allowed us to publish the entire sequence in the journal *Nature* ahead of The Human Genome Project's completion.

Instead of getting let go like some of my colleagues, my productivity positioned me with the ability to decide when my science career would end, or so I thought…

On the domestic side, home life presented difficult challenges. In our first few years of marriage, Mindy endured a confusing array of health problems. Through the trial and error of stumbling through a rigid HMO, specialists finally determined that she had Lupus, an autoimmune disease where the immune system attacks healthy organs and tissue. The disease, aggressive at times, did not lend to her being an equitable partner. My wife contributed what she could, but additional earnings were minimal, so I had to diversify areas of income in order to thrive in an expensive Denver market.

I had started a janitorial business that cleaned commercial offices in the evenings. Cleaning provided a steady source of supplemental income that also allowed me to be flexible with my time. On top of that, I had taken a part-time position working with teenagers at our local, non-denominational church, where I learned to revere the art of storytelling and metaphor.

My life, and my twenties in particular, were full. My career in the laboratory kept me intellectually stimulated, and it never felt like work. Serving in the church won me a reputable stature in our community. My janitorial company added lucrative accounts as I applied the same principles of technique, efficiency, and care that I did in other areas of life. Although not overtly cognizant of my ego, I did have small pockets of awareness of how

I spoke to people about my position and standing when it came to achievements. If my audience was conservative, I'd let them know I was a pastor. With a more progressive audience, I would talk science. If it benefitted a conversation, I was an entrepreneur. When Mindy's Lupus would flare, I became a nurse, a mom. I derived my value from being keenly aware of what another's needs and expectations were, and then delivering to them the person I needed to be.

I had little desire or compulsion towards alcohol in my early to mid-twenties. I chased with passionate proficiency the goodness being cultivated in my world. If I purchased a six-pack of beer for Thanksgiving, one or two were consumed and the other four or five would hang around, getting pushed to the back of the fridge until New Year's. On my birthday, I could take it or leave it, especially on a workday. Drinking was presented, not pursued... Super Bowls, camping, vacations, and holidays... That was it.

I remember, though, a distinct moment when things started to change. It didn't strike me at the time, but when we settled into our final house and neighborhood, I started applying my highly observational and agreeable nature to our community. Neighbors would pull out their lawn chairs, park them on the sidewalk, and watch the kids play in the cul-de-sac, drinking and socializing with regularity. Strong friendships were being built, and I was more than happy to fall in line. Even though my alcohol use in the past had been minimal, I longed for the communal nature of hanging out with cherished friends. In a way, I had simply applied the formula that had allowed me to be successful in work and family to our community environment. My surroundings and opportunities changed, and so would I. I eagerly morphed into a more consistent drinker.

Weekends were designed in lockstep with drinking. There was an almost competitive nature to luring friends to one another's homes to drink. Morris had a full theater with a bar and an assortment of expensive scotch. Scott had a pool table in his three-car garage. Jared had a kegerator and hung a flag off his front porch to signal happy hour. Our home boasted a hot tub and a dimly lit basement we called the Olive Room. If you wanted sophisticated wine and a killer collection of music on vinyl, you went to Mitchell and Amy's, and so on… Our kids would play, and we would drink and commune into the early morning hours, bouncing to one another's homes like we were changing music stages at a festival.

In my late twenties, trips to the liquor store were becoming more frequent. I remember one afternoon, Mindy and I swung into our city's warehouse-style liquor store, Bubbles. I had a six-pack of beer in my hand when we turned the corner of the aisle and bumped into a cart teeming with every type of booze imaginable. The cart almost looked like an overflowing hodgepodge containing a collection of clearance items.

I raised my head to say excuse me. Behind the cart stood our church's worship leader and her husband. Now, for an increasingly accepting alcohol culture that has slogans on baby's onesies that say, "Mom's Drinking Buddy" or yoga apparel that reads "Day Drinker," let's just say that alcohol consumption in the Christian church remained a little taboo. It was probably on par with masturbation; you know others are probably doing it, but you are not going to tell anyone, let alone do it together. Metaphorically, the youth pastors and worship leaders had been caught with their pants down.

We exchanged uncomfortable hellos, drawing out the greeting long enough to try and think of something else to say.

Finally, Mindy joked, "Well, since it looks like you guys know how to have fun too, you should invite us over sometime! Looks like you'll have enough!"

They quickly let us know that they host a large New Year's Eve party. We parted ways, giggling, thankful that we separated our interaction on the six-pack side of moderation and not the wheelbarrow of shame.

A veiled secret had been lifted, allowing us to graft them into our most trusted friends. So much so that a handful of us from the church, including them, decided to just start meeting at our house on Saturday nights instead of going to church at all. A few of our more forward-thinking church members grappled with the embarrassment of how organized church was compartmentalized from the rest of the community. We thought that living, eating, singing, and talking about meaningful truths (and drinking) should all be done in the same place. All of our neighbors would be welcomed to our in-house gathering: young, old, gay, straight, divorced, atheist. It didn't matter who you were; you would be loved and accepted.

So, after a decade of hustle, striving in multiple disciplines of work, parenting Nathan, juggling all of the paternal and many of the maternal duties, we had cultivated the perfect billboard for suburban, middle-class living. Early Friday afternoon would start with a motorcycle ride alongside Scott. We'd head to a pub for a few beers and talk about the workweek and the kids, maybe throw some darts. We'd return home to play pool in his garage, while others would start filing in, eagerly cracking their first drink before they greeted you with a hug. Music and laughter would fill the evening air well into the morning.

Saturdays would be much of the same, as a handful of church friends would begin the evening at our house, filling our countertops with food and our refrigerator with drinks. Some nights you'd have ladies drinking wine on the back porch, listening to The Shins with candles going, while two houses over the guys had ordered the Pay-Per-View fights.

It felt perfect. It was tribal, knowing you were safe in the acceptance of your friends. It was trust, having someone lean on you as they confide that the doctor is suggesting antidepressants. It was sacrificial, collecting money to fill the gap for a mortgage during the economic collapse. Our community was sacred. We were in harmony, and alcohol was the conductor.

There was a particular weekend evening that prompted a more festive tone than usual. Morris had received a significant promotion, persuading us to leave the neighborhood to celebrate. We headed into town to finish the night at a bar in the city. Four of us had piled into one vehicle. We had one reluctant group member who agreed to be responsible for not drinking and for driving us home. The night continued at the bar with all the frivolities of laughter, karaoke, and celebratory beers with Jägerbombs.

As last call presented itself and we realized that the night had turned into yesterday, our designated driver let us know that she had had too much to drink to drive us back. We thought better of heading all the way home and decided to go a couple miles down the road to have coffee and eat breakfast instead. My people-pleasing, codependent, take-care-of-the-world nature kicked in and offered to drive us to the breakfast spot. The executive center of my brain was wiped, but my ego, that emboldened sidekick wanting to take care of everyone and save the world, was lit.

We didn't make it down the road to the restaurant. My soul sank into the pit of my stomach as the blue and red flashing lights interrupted our plans to wind down our celebration.

Not heavily intoxicated enough to forget, but easily over the driving limit, I remember every detail from the moment I looked into the rearview mirror to when Mindy picked me up from jail. This wasn't me. This couldn't happen to me, right? I had curated such a careful and calculated world where I was the person who made all the right moves. I had the right job, we had the right income, my son went to the right charter school... My house even faced the right direction, so I never had to shovel snow.

I remember lying on the carpet the next day with Mindy, watching a movie—our escape. But I could not have been further from the storyline. My mind was chasing all of the unknowns of how my future would be affected by my DUI. What do I have to do now? Do I need a lawyer? Will they look at my spotless record and let me go? Did the police do anything wrong so I might get off? When will my blood alcohol content come back? Should I get a suit for court?

Isolated and alone in my mind, with an endless number of answerless questions, the phone rang.

"Hello?"

Morris, a respectable, high-ranking military officer, was on the other end. "Jeff, how are you doing? Listen, man, I am so sorry. I want to let you know, and nobody else knows, but this happened to me last year. I feel awful. I knew better than to put myself in that situation again, but I let you do it. I'm sorry. I should have said something. I just... I guess I was looking out for myself."

I paced the hallway, somber and contrite, but not angry. As cordial and caretaking as ever, I said, "It wasn't your fault. I should have known better. Stupid."

It felt comforting to have an advocate. I wasn't alone. Furthermore, I wasn't a fuck-up. Something like this can happen to the best of us, even a lieutenant colonel.

Morris gave me a rundown of the legal process, the hoops I would have to jump through, and the likely consequences. He assured me that the path through this mistake would be an inconvenient pain in the ass, like an IRS audit, but that the authorities didn't want to destroy you; mostly, they just wanted to take from you.

That same summer, Dr. David Bauer invited me to his laboratory to update me on his progress in the field of adult stem cell differentiation. Stem cells are a primary, primitive cell that contain all of your DNA, but none of it has been translated into what type of cell or healthy tissue it will become. Being able to differentiate and "turn on" adult stem cells was a novel and highly sought after Holy Grail in the molecular genetics field, primarily because our bodies are populated with adult stem cells and it eliminates the need to research fetal stem cells, a highly controversial and forbidden technique at the time.

A few years prior, when Dr. Bauer and I were colleagues, we had published a paper on a small peptide that activated stem cells, a discovery that would not only have implications for a wide-reaching spectrum of diseases but could also have a significant effect on the understanding of aging itself.

I remained somewhat of a free agent when it came to laboratories that I could work in. My janitorial company afforded me a stable income and I no longer required the money gained from working in the genetics field. I had taken some time off from the sciences to focus on my company, my wife's health, and our community. Itching for the right project to lure me back in, Dr. Bauer's pitch sparked my senses to return to doing what I really loved. I felt like working in the lab and pushing the envelope in the biomedical field was my highest calling and the one that brought me the most fulfillment. Dr. Bauer had spent the last two years filing patents and proof of concept papers on our peptide. He had bounded over administrative hurdles and drafted many grant applications in order to generate additional money to continue our work.

He was ready to have me back. We toured the laboratory as he explained what the next steps in our research would try to accomplish. He saddled me up on the new Laser Confocal Microscope, an instrument more expensive than a top-of-the-line Porsche, where we could unveil whether our peptide-treated stem cells would differentiate into healthy neurons. We pored over our lab notebooks and former techniques. My eyes danced across the pages of progress, intensifying my yearning to reboot my molecular biology career. Ending the meeting, we projected a rough timeline for when the grant money would appear and I would begin.

That late summer, and into autumn, I was almost beside myself with anxiety watching two massive shipping freighters slowly heading for collision. One carried the weight of a single night's mistake, a stupid decision of drinking too much, driving a car, and getting a DUI. It carried the weight of losing my driver's license, financial windfalls, community service, rigid therapy, and court-designated class schedules. It also carried fear, shame, and anxiety in response to the constant reminders of your mistake.

The other shipping freighter carried all of the opportunity and bliss that stimulated my talents and passions. It had all the potential of completing groundbreaking and innovative work in the sciences, promising a lifetime of accomplishments that I could be proud of.

A month later, as I walked down my driveway, ready to leave for my first day back in the lab, I should have had a more anticipatory excitement in my step... but I didn't. I sat in my car and the overwhelming reality of what I was about to undergo from the correctional system hit me. My judgments had been levied. I was going to start this job, and three weeks later, I would lose my license. I didn't have the means to make it to work any other way, as our suburban home sat 40 miles from the university. Even if I did, I also had weekly group therapy classes to attend, and community service during business hours. I considered being honest with Dr. Bauer, but my stubbornness in not displaying any outward character defects prevented me.

The conflict was overwhelming. I soothed my pride, emboldening my ego that if I just continued being a business owner and taking care of my family, then that would be a noble purpose too. I could justify continuing to get Nathan ready for school, expanding our business so we had solid health insurance for Mindy, and focusing on learning to be a better leader in our church. Furthermore, the consequences were not so steep that I had to let everyone know. I would be able to maintain my life with the same respect and fun communal activities that had already been cultivated.

I sat, defeated, affixed to our driveway. Slowly, I methodically looped the car key ring around my index finger, like a metronome bouncing back and forth between opportunity and consequence. Realizing that the deadening of anxiety was only allowing short sips of breath, like a caged animal, I sighed.

I picked up my phone, called Dr. Bauer, and told him I could no longer accept the research position.

And so it proved true in my case that no hero's legendary journey ever starts with, "And so he left the driveway."

Chapter 3
The Suburbs

11:25 AM

Waiting for a young mother who was pulling her toddler in a plastic wagon across the threshold of our driveway, I slid our Jeep into reverse. I squeezed Tammy's thigh with my thumb and forefinger, as we started creeping through the neighborhood.

I'm not certain that couples should ever have to go into a therapist's office. That isn't to say that they don't need counseling; they just don't need to go into the office. All that could be learned about how partners interact could more easily be observed by setting up a dash-cam in the direction of the driver and passenger for a couple of hours and then uploading the video to a mental health professional.

I cherish road trips with Tammy. It is the data point that specifically assures me that I am in love, and not only that I am in love, but that I actually *like* being with her. I don't loathe lengthy close-proximity situations.

I don't look for reasons to maintain separate schedules. I eagerly anticipate our time together, and if a dash-cam were pointed at us in our car, it would not be recording a lot of negative micro-expressions.

We drove out of our neighborhood, observing the activity of the weekend hustle and bustle. Where most of the homes were newly built and architecturally similar, new neighbors tried to put their individual stamp on their new property as they filled in their landscaping. Children played on the dirt mounds of vacant lots and the occasional contractor's truck would block the road and visibility. A certain relief and sense of accomplishment flushes me as I recall the amount of effort I had put into fixing up our yard. Being in my early forties, doing it myself had taxed me physically, but the payoff was tremendous. Every day that I had worked on the yard that summer carried a jolt of gratitude that I was alive and active, physically healthy, and not preoccupied with drinking the night before.

As we headed towards the highway, we checked to see if we were both comfortable and if the temperature is right. We came to a consensus of what we'd like to listen to, always sensitive to the styles of music or podcasts we put on. It helps that we have ridiculously similar tastes. I know and can rap every word to The Humpty Dance, and she knows when to circle her shoulders as the bass line rolls around the car. Tammy can sing every word to Salt-N-Pepa's "Shoop" and indulges me with the male's cameo verse at the end. She lets me butcher the words with bravado that I am "six-foot-three and have a hot rod, 12 inches like a yard and have you sounding like a reta--."

She quieted the music after our powerful rap duo dies down. "You can't say that anymore."

"What, that I'm six-three? Have I been shrinking? Hopefully, you're not talking about the 12-inch thing?"

"No, the r-word."

"I didn't say it. I mouthed it. My voice just sounds so similar and deep that the recording sounded exactly like me."

This set us on a course of conversation about the history of things we could say and watch in the past that we shouldn't say or do anymore. We had philosophical conversations about inappropriate content like Speedy Gonzales cartoons and whether they should be posted on YouTube. This trailed into a discussion about censorship and why stand-up comedy gets a hall pass to be offensive.

Without much thought, I offered that the Speedy Gonzalez cartoons horribly portrayed the Mexican mice, lying up against a building, drunk, and that they undoubtedly enforced negative stereotypes.

Tammy, with a more thought out and heavier handed explanation, argued that the whole premise of the cartoon was flat out racist. "The whole idea that the only superpower that a Mexican needs to appease the other Mexicans is that he is quicker than they are. Horrible. Fast? That's the superpower? White people get flight, laser beam eyes, but all the Mexican has to do is run a 5K faster than his friends?"

Our time together is never dull. We are comfortable learning from one another. We can unveil insecurities and we uphold honesty, no matter what, as our highest virtue. I feel safe in her company, always.

We navigated the heavier concrete-laden, midday traffic of Colorado Springs. The area has grown exponentially, as the wood, brick, and metal structures try to compete with the 14,000-foot Pikes Peak and the surrounding mountains that towered over the city. We exited onto a southern off ramp that would take us into the suburbs and foothills for a more scenic journey. There were quicker ways to get to the castle, but escaping civilization presented the more serene option.

A moment of conversational pause caused me to turn the music back up. We had accumulated a wonderful playlist of driving music over the last seven years.

Vetting our musical tastes had delivered moments of trial and error in the past. I would try and sneak on some Rage Against the Machine, only to be gently reminded by Tammy that we were white people living in one of the top ten most expensive counties in America.

Likewise, she had tried playing Daughtry and I would have to look over my shoulder playfully.

"What's wrong?" she asked.

"I was checking to see if there were any kids in the car and why we were listening to music that sounds like it was written by a third grader?"

With courteous consideration for one another's critiques, those bands lie on the cutting room floor. What remains is an eccentric curation of all genres of music.

As I turned up the music, the upbeat, blaring Motown-style horns accompanied Nathaniel Rateliff & The Night Sweats screaming, "Son of a bitch!" in a song where the singer intensely yells for someone to give him a drink.

This deceptively catchy song, "S.O.B.," was popularized a couple of years ago and has become an anthem for many folks who celebrate the chorus and the happy, jazzy sound, but who can't read between the lines.

It is reminiscent of the late Amy Winehouse and her upbeat, throwback style, singing, "No," when they tried to take her back to rehab.

The music has a high, blissful tempo that masks the darkness underneath.

Nathaniel Rateliff is a local musician in Denver and has been performing in various bands since the early 2000s. I was a fan well before the single "S.O.B." launched him into everyone's household.

He is one of those artists whose very words seemed to park themselves right into your same situation. In the case of Mr. Rateliff and myself, the meaning and passion portrayed through "S.O.B." went well past the explosive plea for a drink. The song was about a relationship nearing its end.

◻˝F ₿ €˝◻

The summer after I decided not to return to the sciences was a time of keeping my head down and observing the terms of my DUI. I had staffed and stocked up my cleaning company so that it would not need my attention while I navigated life with restricted mobility. Once the DMV reinstated my license, I had strict usage requirements that only allowed me to go to and from work and to get Nathan back and forth from school.

I peppered my daytime hours with court-ordered community service and group therapy classes, which I actually enjoyed. I met a diverse subset of people from all walks of our community. Of course, we had a few degenerate fuck-ups that you could point to and say, "Well, I'm certainly not like them."

We also had upstanding, functional members in those classes, like Paul, who traveled and contracted with Microsoft. Dianne ran a reputable temporary staffing agency in a nearby city. Dan, who lived in the nicest area in town, received his DUI picking up his daughter from gymnastics in the evening after a few glasses of wine. There were many people just like me, responsible people in our community who felt like they shouldn't be punished. Drinking and driving had been a lapse in judgment and not a chronic occurrence.

Our overarching theme: problem drinking didn't cause our circumstances. As we created our narrative, it went something like this: the county and the court systems function on the revenue they obtain from DUI charges. It is predicated, therefore, on the authorities putting you into the system so that they can get your money. Done.

I can't solidly remember extending weekend-only drinking into imbibing on weeknights, but I'm fairly sure that it happened around this time. Trying to keep a DUI under wraps, but having the logistical hurdles ever before you, created its own type of anxiety and shame that you wanted to escape from. I categorized the system as the villain, not the alcohol. The alcohol would call you with all the promises of making the increased stressors go away.

Our weekends continued to look similar to what they had before: neighbors gathered, and we drank. Since Mindy and I always hosted the Saturday gathering, a stockpile of left-behind liquor collected in our home.

Weekdays became different. I had trimmed responsibilities away from my cleaning company due to having a restricted license, and I had reluctantly and with great pain decided not to continue my work in the biomedical sciences. Preparations for our small in-home church meeting required minimal preparation throughout the week. Overall, I just had more downtime... boredom.

With my evening janitorial duties completed, I would arrive home to a quiet household. With Nathan and Mindy tucked in bed on the upper level, I would settle in with a beer and answer emails to staff and clients. One beer would turn into two, and I would feel the loneliness break, as the alcohol would wrap my insides with a warm, soft hug. Since I had the computer going, I would listen to an audio teaching or maybe do some writing. As the drinks increased, intellectual pursuits decreased, redirecting the computer to YouTube videos or retro porn.

Bathroom trips were more frequent now, and so were trips to the kitchen. I'd decide on a cocktail after searching to see what our church friends had left behind... *I'll get fat if I drink too much beer.* Smaller cocktails would turn into double pours... *I don't want to want to wake anyone up by turning the light on multiple times... Be careful that the sound of the bottle doesn't clink when putting it back.*

One more cocktail would accompany me to the hot tub, alone, but happy. I would finish the late evening by setting my phone alarm to Nathan's wake time, tossing the phone on the coffee table out of reach. *Rolling Stone* would accompany me on the couch, telling me a story that was not my own, teasing me to always think outward, never in, until I'd drift away.

This became my quiet routine, burying my feelings. I didn't stagger around the house or want to play music too loud. I didn't belligerently wake up Mindy and ask her why we hadn't slept in the same bed for over a decade or why she was able to make it to fitness classes but not to contribute with the carpool kids. I didn't air out any grievances of my dissatisfactions with the household and workloads, making the meals, and running a company. I never outwardly expressed that I had originally left the sciences because the company made more money and she kept wanting nicer things.

It never helped to air my resentments. It always came back to ill-treatment during childhood, or how sick she was with Lupus. I felt like a monster if I requested a more equitable and loving relationship from someone who ended any confrontation with, "I am who I am. I'm doing the best I can."

I pleaded during our first few years of marriage for more reciprocal care, but a suicide scare was the result. If the weight of your partner's life is on you, you just do what you've always done: you read the room, determine what the need is, and then deliver. In our 16-year marriage, I delivered passivity. I delivered silence. No arguments and no contentious bickering. I put my hands to the plow and did it with a smile.

Neither of us would have characterized ourselves as unhappy. We just became comfortable occupying separate space. We'd come together on the occasional evening to binge watch a full season of a show or to celebrate a holiday or a family member's birthday. She had her interests (religion, fitness classes) and I had the business, chores, and friendships. It seemed normal, and if not incredibly vibrant and loving between the two of us, at least it felt safe. My disposition in our relationship was the same as it was anywhere: find the need and accomplish it. In that way, I could be valuable, safe, and respected. Respectability was the currency I valued in every area of life.

Increasingly, though, in the year after my DUI, Mindy and a friend had been going to downtown Denver for weekend activities instead of hanging out with the neighborhood friends. It didn't bother me. I had always felt secure in our relationship. Mindy was always complimentary, offering me solid words of affirmation. I was quite secure in myself, as well, given that I valued productivity and so was an industrious contributor within our marriage. Her leaving our core group on the weekends wasn't a big deal and I trusted her. Moreover, she wasn't just moderately religious, but zealous, which seemed to provide a moral safety net from wrongdoing. In addition, I had harnessed a degree of indifference, because I was thoroughly entertained by our neighborhood and our alcohol-fueled ongoings.

Prior to Thanksgiving, I had started dabbling in trail running as a hobby. It would be an understatement to say that I didn't have the fitness bug as a lifelong passion like Mindy did. Still, I had increasingly taken to the open park spaces near our home. Traditionally, I would have to be tricked into exercise: roller hockey, ultimate frisbee, tennis. In trail running, there was a welcome distraction, navigating the trails and enjoying nature. I found it fun and competitive to enter the occasional 5K race with Mindy. It was an opportunity to meet her where she was at with her allegiance to fitness, and it allowed us to do something together.

That year, we had entered our city's Thanksgiving Day Turkey Trot, a 5K race that benefited local food banks. The night before the race seemed very similar to what our normal Fridays had become. Friends entered into the neighborhood with a festive and anticipatory attitude towards a four-day weekend. Mindy had decided to go out with her friend Jill while the rest of us hung back and primed our weekend with a few drinks. I didn't go overboard with drinking that night, committed to bringing my race time down.

As I awoke on Thanksgiving morning to prepare for the race, I went upstairs to see if Mindy was getting ready. The bed was still made, the bathroom empty. I checked the garage for her car. Nothing. I tried her phone, which went directly to voicemail.

It was awkward, but not alarming. I figured that her phone was dead and that, since a fitness event was more her thing than mine, we would probably see each other at the race. I headed out to the county fairgrounds.

I approached the registration tables, wading through a sea of people, their cold, early morning breath expelling cackles of jokes about the massive amounts of food they would have license to eat later in the day. My neck craned, head bobbing, looking for that one familiar smile, but still no Mindy. Worry competed with irritation, but I was committed and already there, so I took a quick stretch and ran the race in 23 minutes.

I tried her again on her phone afterwards. She picked up. "Sorry. We had a late night, and we couldn't drive. We stayed at a friend's loft in LoDo. My phone died. I'm at home getting ready now. We have to be at your Mom's at noon. Jeff, I am so, so sorry... How was the race?"

I swallowed my feelings and hid them behind small talk. My relief that she was okay quickly turned into annoyance at being shunned doing something that was closer to her area of interest. I was meeting her in her arena to get closer, but in her neglect of the race, it signaled my position in her list of priorities.

As I drove home from the race, I wasn't just angry about the morning. I gripped the steering wheel tight, angry about everything, all the feelings I'd been drinking to bury and the disappointments that I lacked the courage to address. Her not showing up for the race embodied the whole microcosm in our marriage, of her not showing up for me at all.

The drive to my parents' house for Thanksgiving dinner started eerily quiet. Nathan, all of eight years old, had his DVD player with headphones in, keeping noise to a minimum. My stern focus on the road could easily have been mistaken for intentionally icing Mindy out of a conversation, but me being able to voice displeasure always came at the cost of some sort of guilt trip. If she got stressed out or was confronted with wrongdoing, she could go into a Lupus flare, or I'd be blamed for her having to take an additional benzo or sleeping pill later that day. Honest conversation had never produced a result that was worth the guilt.

The truth is, the whole situation was an anomaly, her not coming home, and I didn't feel threatened as much as I was offended that she didn't care enough to prioritize *our* thing.

Mindy broke our silence, easing in, "Jeff, I'm getting scared. I think we should start sleeping in the same bed."

I reactively jerked my head back in surprise like I was dodging a fastball thrown up and in. Looking back to see that Nathan couldn't hear, I said, "What? Uhhh... I don't disagree, but where is this coming from?"

"I don't know... I mean, like I said, I'm getting scared. I'm starting to think about being with other people... I haven't... Know that I haven't, but I've been thinking about it and I think we need to do figure out something different."

My discernment kicked in; the intuition in the pit of my stomach knew. Something had happened.

I kept driving, silent, stunned. Tears welled up in my eyes and I shook my head in disappointment.

Surprisingly, the offense of her being with someone else, or even considering it, wasn't what stung. That she had any passion at all in that direction leveled me curious. But the ease and injustice of her so freely being able to communicate what was happening in her world, her areas of interest or dissatisfaction, left the scales so unevenly tipped. How was it that I felt I had to bury everything, and she could, after already disregarding our morning event, casually drop in an elusively worded conversation about infidelity... on the drive to Thanksgiving dinner?

Instead of instituting my passive and agreeable nature to fall in line with her course of conversation, I used whatever uneasiness she felt to learn more. "What's been going on downtown when you're going out with Jill? What are you feeling?"

"I don't know. I'm 35 but feel like I'm going on 25 and there's a whole world of people doing things out there that I want to experience. We got married so young. I just feel like I've missed so much."

In a mild tone, I suggested, "You know, you don't have to miss out. You can go."

She paused, calculating the weight of my offer. "You mean divorce?"

"I mean, we remain friends. That's all we've ever been, anyway, is friends. Go live your life the way you want to live it. I'd like to continue living mine. I like my life and don't need be out there doing anything else."

As we drove, I talked somewhat dispassionately, surgically, but kindly. Mindy did the same. A catatonic, disbelieving air settled around us as 16 years of marriage wound down in a single car ride. We pulled into the driveway.

We sat for a second, knowing that Nathan would either start dismounting to enter towards Grandma and Grandpa's or that they would come out to greet us. Mindy's voice tremored as she said, "So we're getting a divorce?"

I stole a quick peek in the rearview mirror, Nathan's headphones were still neatly attached over his ears. I released my seatbelt. Stoic and trying to harness the appearance of devastation in front of my parents, I said, "Yeah. I think we're done."

◻ʺℲ ฿ Ɔʺ◻

Tammy and I traversed north to south through the first outcropping of foothills towards the upper mountains. The road gradually climbed the surrounding landscape, which boasted a blend of desert-like, unimpressive hills that were sparse with trees and dry from the late summer drought. After 45 minutes, we slowed up upon a cross-section where the state highways would intersect. Creeping towards the intersection revealed a weathered truck stop and a few outbuildings along with a large hand-painted billboard that read: **RUSTY for SHERIFF**.

"I feel like if I was committing a crime, I would want the Sheriff's name to be Rusty. Rusty seems like he'd be slow. But, if I had some land that needed protecting, that name wouldn't inspire me."

Tammy asked, "So, *are you or are you not* voting for Rusty?"

"I don't know," I mused. "I don't own any land out here and, technically, he's not my sheriff. Since I'm not certain whether *we will or will not* commit a crime today, I think it's best that I hypothetically vote for him."

We crossed the intersection continuing south. I had a brief moment where I realized that I was working off of my mental GPS from staring at the map in bed earlier. That would do for the moment. I could have easily punched the address into navigation before we left, but not using a $30,000 rolling computer added more mystery.

As the music continued to shuffle on our playlist, our anthem from when we first met started firing intro guitar licks. Blue October's "She's My Ride Home" narrated us meeting each other, both carrying damage and disappointments from past relationships, and leaving them behind. I reached down to boost the volume a bit higher. The lyrics blistered through our car, describing the act of pouring gas on our history, lighting a match, and watching it go up in flames through the rearview window.

Straight after the intersection, the highway started heading downwards a bit. Tammy raised her hands in the air like she was riding rollercoaster. She made sure I could hear, "Weeeeeeee!" over the music. We do this often. It is our affirmation that we are loving this wild ride... and if you could mount a dash-cam on the front of our amusement ride, our life, I'm certain that our imaginary therapist would be pleased.

Chapter 4

The Jail

12:45 PM

Our quest leisurely wound us down into the Arkansas River Valley as we approached the small, one-lane town of Florence, Colorado. Small, single-level, brick storefronts lined the main street with a hardware store and some antique shops. Whereas just a half-hour prior, my foot on the gas pedal had kept in time with our music, indifferent to speed limit signs, I now quickly came in tune with the heavy number of County and State Patrol vehicles using this small town as their hub.

In my heaving drinking days, visible sightline of an officer would throw me into a reactionary posture. I would ask Tammy to move her feet from the dash. I would wonder if all of my taillights were working. I didn't want to get pulled over. Any police officer could punch in my license and see that I had a record, a record that would automatically tip them off to inquire further as to whether I was under the influence of alcohol. And truth be told, whether it was a fog from the night before or traces of booze that had not metabolized, I was never quite sure whether I was or not.

But my posture is different now, relaxed. My heart rate did not increase; I did not get the innate urge of fight or flight that used to indiscriminately pull my brain's levers. I am free. I breezed past the officers as if daring them to check me out, almost wanting them to validate the work that I had done in getting sober.

Tammy and I swung into the town's nicest gas station, knowing that we'd prefer not to add to our adventure by running out of fuel. As I began to engage the pump, I couldn't help but watch Tammy stride into the small gas station market. She is tall and pretty, and if you only saw the sophisticated outside, you wouldn't understand the childlike inner workings of her approaching a gas station. On a road trip, she's like a kid with a $5 bill being sent into the dollar store, the aisles of snacks her Mecca.

I waved to tell her I'd be in. Maybe she thought that was my way of policing her quantity of Slim Jim purchases, but truly, in my own childlike way, I wanted to see what kind of creative concoction I could make out of their coffee machine.

The inside of the gas station mirrored the outside of the town. There were many uniformed officers, some sitting at the adjoining Subway eating sandwiches. Mental pings of confidence coursed through my mind, small benchmarks reminding me that I no longer lived with inner terror. I could respectfully nod in their direction, boasting through the whites of my eyes.

Tammy and I left the town, having made our signature financial deposit, not coming away empty handed. We continued our journey, heading slightly east at the main intersection, with an assortment of coffees, sunflower seeds, jerky, and sandwiches.

Just a few miles out of town, an enormous brick structure drew our heads to the left of the landscape. The open ranch spaces and gigantic mountains of the Arkansas River Valley were blasphemed by this unsightly manmade structure. As we got closer, we could identify the tall chain-link fence and razor wire. The reason for the excessive number of uniformed officers we'd seen became clear: it was a prison. The Florence Supermax Penitentiary... The Alcatraz of the Rockies.

I guess we shouldn't have been surprised. This whole area of the Rocky Mountains is dotted with prisons. Canyon City, the biggest city west of here, has been known internationally for housing our nation's worst inmates.

In these moments, I like to think that some of our demographic stereotypes, derived out of expanding the west, are true. If people who stayed on the east coast during the pioneer days are characterized as being unadventurous and stubborn, and the folks who made it all the way to California during the Gold Rush are thought of as energetic and ambitious, I like to think that people who settled in Colorado are somewhere in the middle. Maybe even like me: passive and agreeable. I can picture the pioneers coming up against the western mountain range, 14,000-foot mountains sprawling left to right as far as the eye can see, and saying, "Uh… We're good. Let's settle here."

"But Pa, what about the gold in California?"

"We'll settle for silver. My hemorrhoids *will not* be going over those mountains."

Likewise, maybe that's why they tuck all of these prisons within the mountains. If a prisoner broke through the two-foot-thick walls and bypassed three stages of fence and razor wire, he'd look up at the Rocky Mountains he had to go over and say, "Oh, fuck that. Let me back in!"

But more than the subjective musings most people have in passing such a foreign place, my thoughts strayed a little deeper… I know what it's like to be on the inside.

◦ "F ₿ €" ◦

I didn't really have a strong reference for what divorce was supposed to look like. I came from a two-parent family home, my only sister's first marriage remained intact, and our inner circle of friends were solidly together. My church group leaned on the side of reconciliation at all costs.

What I did know of divorce was that it could be pretty nasty. Partners on each side tend to prop themselves up, often falsely, portraying themselves as the more important person.

We waited until after the holidays to tell Nathan that we were getting divorced, not wanting his eight-year-old mind to forever associate Christmas with his parents' separation. To his knowledge, we were going as a family to the recreation center to spend the afternoon swimming. Even though we would be levying traumatic news, we wanted this to be offset by the counter-experience that Mindy and I were still friends and that we would continue doing family events together as a team.

Beforehand, Mindy and I sat in our master bedroom and prayed together for the last time. I'll admit, my prayer was disingenuous. I mean, there is a way in which you are praying to God, and there is a whole other way you use prayer to indirectly speak to the other person in the room. I was doing the latter…

"Lord, we know that Nathan is ultimately in your hands. We pray that the plans you have for him, his destiny, is not affected by our mistakes, our shortcomings. We pray that he is resilient and knows that our love for him is our most important priority. Even though we head in different directions from one another, please continue to soften our hearts and guide our actions that we may always find a way to put him first."

Then we called Nathan up to our bedroom. His bubbly innocence popped through the double doors. I pulled up a chair next to the window while Mindy remained on the bed. He split the space between us.

I started, "Buddy, have you ever walked up to a glass of water, certain that it was water, but when you tasted it, it was actually Sprite?"

"Yeah! It kinda freaks you out a little bit and then you're happy it's soda."

"Your mom and I have something to tell you…"

It was brutal. It cored out our spirits. We spoke in endearing tones. We all cried together. We gave assurances that his home, school, and friends would remain the same.

Mindy crept down from the bed and the three of us hugged tight.

With Nathan's chin quivering and his soggy eyes pulling back from our tight hug, he asked, "We all still get to go swimming, right?"

"Heck yeah!" I said. "Go get your suit on and your big towel. We'll get ready."

Mindy and I stood up and stared into each other's swollen, devastated faces.

"I can't, Jeff. I just can't go like this. I can't. Please, please, you take him."

It's the most disappointment I had ever felt, *ever,* and it was safe to calculate that we wouldn't be going through any jockeying of importance hierarchy.

The conversation in our car on Thanksgiving Day was the reality of what unfolded. We granted her the liberty to try whatever she wanted to try, to create her new world. I retained the house, the business, and Nathan. We didn't use opportunistic lawyers, paid our assets evenly, and we shared custody so that she wouldn't have to pay child support or vice versa if things panned out differently. Poof. Done.

It wasn't difficult for me to preserve an outward look of piety. A mom that didn't prioritize child rearing didn't need to be annotated or falsely denounced. In her defense, she wasn't delusional about her caretaking abilities, and I was thankful for that. It's where I've heard divorces can escalate the worst. We knew that I had been the stabilizing factor for Nathan and would continue to be so. That's really all I wanted. She would fall in line with her time and contributions as she figured out her new course, and she expected him to be in good hands going forward.

In a way, that checked the outer boxes for me, my appearance in the community. I wanted to be the most accomplished scientist in the lab, the orator standing at the front of the church, and to own the house that faces the right direction—those visible signals to others that you know how to make the right choices in life.

But inwardly, I was tortured. I couldn't reconcile how I had let my marriage collapse, when I hadn't even realized it was broken. *How did this happen?* How could acts of service, finding your value in producing and taking care of other people, lead to this—betrayal? Her wanting something else? *Someone* else?

Experts say that drug abuse or alcoholism can be genetic, can be induced by environmental factors, or can be a combination of both. If you have a genetic propensity towards alcoholism, but you are never in an environment to take a drink, you will never experience the symptoms of your condition. If you do not carry a genetic component, but your environment places you in a situation where you drink often enough, neurobiochemistry doesn't give a shit about your genetics. You will become addicted. Enter my spiral.

Prior to our divorce, I had built the routine of drinking in the late evenings. The amount that I drank was in direct proportion to how badly I needed to alter my feelings. In fact, I didn't even realize that this was what I was doing, but I was unknowingly building a habit, quietly burying my resentments. Post-divorce, I not only wanted to alter feelings; I wanted to escape. Escape the responsibilities, escape the shame of failure, and escape the pain of abandonment.

Some of the hardest moments were the ones where my ego broke and I realized the contributions that Mindy *had made*. Wrapping Christmas presents by myself, or paying bills and keeping tight financial records, were other moments when I realized I was not the sacrificial martyr that I had always patted myself on the back for being.

I had arranged to have a nanny come live in one of Nathan's and my spare bedrooms. Our domestic survival relied on having someone in the house in the evening, because most of my business operations took place at night. At any given hour, someone on my cleaning team could call me and need me to come help or rescue them. Given that Nathan was predominantly with me, I obviously couldn't leave an eight-year-old unsupervised. At the same time, I didn't want a live-in nanny to be his parent either, so I continually searched for the balance of me being at home and keeping everything in the business highly predictable.

The conditions of my environment changed and so did my alcohol use. More time at home meant more time to drink. A few drinks in the late evening hours after work transformed into starting with a cocktail after carpool while I was making dinner.

Alcoholism is progressive. In the beginning, you never think that a weekend drink will lead to a weekday drink. You don't know that a late-night drink will beckon you to an early evening drink. You cannot predict that day-drinking on your birthday will open the door to considering day-drinking in general, and in your wildest imagination, you never consider that the soft beep of your refrigerator being left open would sound identical to the vitals monitor in your hospital bed.

The change in environmental factors in my life could not be oversold. It was ironic that Mindy was off trying to reclaim her adolescence, which appeared foolish to the rest of us looking on. In contrast, I felt a childlike rebellion on the inside that said, "Fuck it. Who cares anyway? What's the point of being good, if goodness resulted in being discarded?" I harnessed an attitude of self-pity, which drew me further from any visible stability that others might presume existed.

Less than two months after we finalized our divorce, Mindy asked if we could meet for breakfast. My amenable nature had not been dulled or jaded through our separation, so I agreed.

In short, she wanted to ask for forgiveness. She had been seeing a Christian counselor, and this less-than-qualified individual suggested that she tell me all the details of her infidelity, including the day, time, and person. What was once intuited by me, now became concrete. The most abhorrent thing, though, is that after Mindy described the affair, she relayed that man did not even acknowledge her presence the following day. She managed to tell her former husband of 16 years the circumstances of a one-night stand, and yet make it about how she felt mistreated afterwards? This interaction seemed less about my forgiveness and more about her absolving her guilt. The timing further indicated this. Was it not self-preservation to tell me right after the divorce? Would she have been so humble and contrite, inciting my unknown reaction, before we respectfully divided our time and assets?

Most disturbing was my immediate response, a symbolic micro-example of who I was. I calculated Mindy's needs before I even determined my own. I cared for her. *I didn't feel what I needed to feel; I felt what she needed me to feel.* I told her that I had predicted this and that I had already forgiven her. I said that we should move on. What's past is past. We hugged, but my caretaking posture masked the inner agony that would unfold after I'd had time to process our meeting.

Some evolutionary psychologists link the post-traumatic stress disorder (PTSD) that soldiers feel coming home from battle directly to betrayal. Why some soldiers can be in the same battle and emerge with two different mental outcomes has been a mystery. One hypothesis is that it's the mental state of the soldier prior to combat that makes the difference. A soldier that has a gentle view of the world, or even of himself, as being calm, predictable, or safe is more likely to experience PTSD. When you're not able to predict and therefore prepare yourself for the horrors of what you or another is capable of, and then those horrors occur, it rocks the mental foundation of all that you had believed to be true. It's an internal mental betrayal of all that you had thought safe, at your deepest levels of being.

I'm not one to self-diagnose, and I don't even love clinical terms, but I get it. Betrayal rocks the very foundation of all that you thought was true, belief in yourself and belief in humanity. And not only that, but it also makes you second guess yourself as to how you perceive and trust the world afterwards. If fidelity and promises are not real, is God real? Does truth mean anything, or are you constantly setting yourself up by believing anything at all? That is despair.

Mindy didn't break my heart. She broke my truth.

Instead of grappling with the pain of these ideas at the time, I just poured booze over them to make them go away. I didn't want to feel disappointed. I didn't want to feel like I'd been hoodwinked. I didn't want to feel like I'd been a poor judge of character. I didn't want to feel like I had been duped for 16 years into playing a role of big brother, provider, and nurse, instead of a husband, a lover. *I didn't want to feel any of it.*

Going forward, I easily found affirmation that I was desirable by other partners. I always made it a point to park my car during school pick-up and walk inside to get Nathan. I could almost feel the eyes and detect the smiles of single moms, tracking me in a different way.

An empty space on the bleachers during Nathan's basketball game left an opening for a new attractive face trying to share solidarity in how bad divorce was. I'd just confirm the reality, that we had processed ours quickly and remained civil.

Once, when I hosted a playdate with a couple of Nathan's schoolmates, a single mom came to pick up her child afterwards. I swear, she talked right past me as she stared up at the vaulted ceilings, mentally measuring what length of curtains would cover the high windows. Her head bobbed, eyes darting throughout the scope of my home like a lifeguard tracking bodies in a wave pool.

I dated an attorney for a while. A handful of years younger than me, in her late twenties, she had ambitions of a new family together that stressed me to the core. All I could equate it with was a disproportioned amount of the new responsibilities, a world I had conditioned myself to know.

I welcomed the affection and desire, though. It revitalized the hole in my ego from never being desired by Mindy, but with a new partner came a new understanding of how my relationship with alcohol was blossoming. I preferred when my girlfriend was gone, so I could drink like I wanted to. An approaching weekend led to arguments about how and where we would spend our time. I always suggested we stay in the neighborhood, so that I could drink safely (although I never stated this explicitly). I became more withdrawn and isolated when she countered with enthusiastic ideas. Withholding consumption on weekday evenings in her presence, led to regular day-drinking when she was gone. I needed to appease what was missing in my body: alcohol.

A year and a half post-divorce, and approaching the holiday season, I had broken off the relationship with the attorney. We stalled at two different levels in life's goals. She could have stepped into a built-in home and family and we might have survived, but her wanting to double up and create it all again seemed too exhausting… and I was exhausted.

Approaching that Christmas and New Year's, I drank… I mean, *I drank*. Released from companionship, and the people-pleasing accountability that accompanied it, it's like I was trying to recover the lost time that my girlfriend had stolen from my drinking. The mornings introduced the new phenomenon of tremoring hands. I started titrating my blood stream with a small nip in the morning, settling my eyes on the stove's clock, knowing that in 15 to 20 minutes I would be fine. I drank to keep my equilibrium tame, like someone that swallows a steady stream of benzos, medicating to feel normal. I was dependent. *I was addicted.*

Realizing these new indicators of dependence, I devised a plan to head to my vacation cabin and sober up while everyone else was ringing in the New Year. I wrapped up my end-of-year business accounting two days early and finished my final cleaning job of the year on December 29th. Instead of heading home and packing for the cabin, I stopped by our local bar for some communal conversation and a little year-end celebration of my own.

My arrogance in thinking I would abstain from alcohol over New Year's, also fostered conflicted feelings I would be missing out in the coming days. I self-celebrated a little too hard at the bar and needed to call our nanny to see if she could come pick me up. After she arrived, she hung out for a bit and had a few drinks of her own.

I didn't really question whether she had had too much to get us home. In fact, my friend Morris had written the playbook on this a few years prior. I put her at risk, so that *I would be safe.* We drove home, laughing and talking about the people we had met at the bar, relishing in silly banter. Instead of wrapping around the sharp left corner in our pristine neighborhood, she continued straight, impaling her mid-sized SUV into a large five-foot decorative boulder in the middle of a neighbor's yard.

I did not spend New Year's Eve sobering up at my cabin. I spent New Year's Eve waking up in the hospital. The addition of new, unintended consequences in my relationship with alcohol were reaching a whole new level. I had six broken bones, the worst of which was an upper leg, femur, and hip fracture where the dashboard had collided with my body. Three broken bones in my hand, a broken nose, and torn ligaments in my neck rounded out the major injuries. Lacerations and indentations in my shins from where the engine block shot under the dash didn't hurt much; they were minor injuries relative to the pain and damage my ego was about to endure.

I remember waking up in the early morning hours the night of the accident. Darkness blanketed my gummy eyes, interrupted only by the twinkle of foreign lights. In my room, the soft sound of a machine competed with the shuffling of a nurse off to my left. I turned to lo—.

"Please, don't move your head," she said softly. "You've been in an accident. The brunt of the impact was on your side."

A tear rolled down my cheek, wicking from my chin into my neck brace. "Shit, I'm still here," I whispered with defeated sadness.

"I'm sorry, what was that?"

"Nothing." Keenly aware, I didn't want her to know what I meant.

An abrupt clunking sound pierced the early morning stillness. My eyes shifted to the commotion of a wheelchair prying its way into my room, the silhouette bringing light from the hallway into my darkened room. "Ninja?"

"Miss, you can't be—"

"Oh, Ninja!" Our nanny rolled in and disregarded the nurse. "I'm so sorry. I can't... I... I thought you were dead." She cried out, scanning my body. "You weren't moving at all and I..."

"Miss, you can't... This is not the time..."

I remained still. I couldn't intercede. I scoffed at the idea of her endearing nickname, Ninja. Taken from a song we both liked, she'd say, "You're like a ninja, the way you smoothly move in and out of all these different roles you play."

She wheeled herself up, leaning out of the chair to grab my hand. I knew that I had put her in our situation. I had known better. "Tanya, I... How are you? Are you okay?"

"My ankle and wrist are pretty jacked, but nothing like this." She looked me over and sobbed. "I had to see you. I'm so glad you're alive."

I couldn't move to comfort her, and I couldn't share in her sentiment.

While I had intended to sober up over the New Year's weekend, I had not intended to do it in the hospital. The pain in my body was tolerable. The eyes of friends and family standing over my bed, darting over my hapless body, the looks of pity… that was excruciating. *Were they disappointed?* Looks of shame and half-smiles that encouraged me to get better… *Do they know that this wasn't my fault, that I wasn't driving?*

Vulnerability crept through my crippled frame. I had been the person who took care of everyone. I had been the one who had my shit together. I wanted to be as far away from anyone who knew me as possible, yet the leg, hip, and hand braces left me incapable of even using the restroom by myself.

Once the clamor and embarrassment of the first day subsided, my physical insides were screaming at me by late evening. Convinced that I had some internal organ damage, I summoned the nurse. My guts roiled, and I implored the hospital staff to investigate further.

Unable to ignore my concerns, they wheeled me back for an additional MRI in the middle of the night.

Returning from the MRI and settling back into my room, I became nauseous. I told my nurse, "I think I'm going to be sick."

With no time for him to react, I vomited. Not able to move side to side, or sit up, the vomit released and was caught within the neck brace that wrapped under my chin. It funneled inside the brace, trapped, seeping down to my chest.

Interrupting his already rough movements and deep sighs, the nurse looked over at me in disgust. I'll never forget that look. He stopped resituating my cords from our MRI travel and began disassembling my bile-filled neck brace.

He growled in my ear, "We didn't need the MRI to tell us what's wrong with your insides. What's wrong is *you're a drunk.*"

I didn't ask for help again after that. Apparently, I deserved the disdain and judgment. I'd lie there for four additional successive nights, in and out of sleep, feeling the intense pain of the broken bones coupled with uncomfortable tremors, sweats, and what felt like pin pricks in my skin.

On my final day before being released, my sister, a nurse herself, entered my room and stood at the foot of my bed. Next, the same nurse, who had whispered that I was a drunk four nights prior, came in with my discharge papers. With them came a well thought out, but optional, program for outpatient alcohol abuse treatment.

He gave me the sell on the treatment program in the kindest tones, with my sister standing by my side. Earlier, though, he'd already enflamed in me any stubbornness I had left that might have been exhausted.

I stared a hole right back through him, not forgetting the way he had spoken to me in the dark. "I'm ready to go," I said. "This wasn't my fault. I'll be fine."

Alcoholism is characterized as a complex brain disease, a condition that is manifested in repetitive and compulsive use of alcohol, despite negative consequences.

Looking back, I shudder with the knowledge that this accident had not cemented my bottom. What did I have to lose by waving the white flag of defeat right then and there? The jig was up. It's not like I didn't have a full audience of people who cared for me that had just witnessed one of the most horrific consequences of drinking. They would have understood. Some people drink in secret for decades and hide it well enough that they need to *convince* others that they have a problem. Me, I would not have had to convince a soul. My six- to seven-year rendezvous with alcohol, starting in my late twenties and ending at age 35, displayed a textbook downward spiral. I had planned on going to my cabin to sober up anyway; maybe I should've taken this as a sign that some divine instrument had helped me along in the process.

Alcoholism is repetitive and compulsive use, *despite negative consequences.*

My sister had helped me into her car after being wheeled out of the hospital. On the drive home, I don't remember a lot being said. I do remember asking for a cigarette, which was given with automation. As the first pull of nicotine calmed my mind, I started mentally surveying the options of liquor in my home that could soon do the same.

She mentioned that she had set up a room for Nathan at her house and that he could stay for as long as necessary while I got used to getting around and driving with the broken leg and hand… That I should take my time.

When I got home, I just wanted to be alone. The newness of moving with splintered limbs intensified the pain, and although I did need assistance with the very basics, I told anyone and everyone who tried to come over and help me, to leave. On the first day, I clumsily navigated my crutches through the 2,800-square-foot house to search for a drink, the only friend I wanted around for consolation. I made my way down two levels to the basement bar to find it had been emptied without my permission. I hobbled to the upstairs and looked in the cabinet above the fridge. Gone. Maybe in the refrigerator? Nothing.

I raised my crutch and flung it across the kitchen. The foam armpit holder rebounded off of the microwave and headed back towards me. I swiped at the crutch, my pride and stubbornness increasing with every heave of breath. *They don't get to decide. They have no right to decide for me… what I can and can't do! They have no idea what it's like to be me… to live my life… to have my pain… and now this, these injuries? I didn't ask for this. This wasn't my fault!*

I hobbled to my car, leg strapped up to the hip, broken hand navigating the use of the crutch, face battered with deep circles under my eyes, and a head framed with a stifling neck brace, in a pathetic pursuit of the only thing I knew that would calm my insides… alcohol. When I balanced on my one good leg to throw the crutches in the back of my car, I noticed the two brown paper bags on the floor: two unopened handles of vodka. Relief and confusion flooded me all at the same time. Had I been planning on taking those up to the cabin for New Year's? Had I not had a plan to dry out and sober up, or had my plan been to take this curse to a fatal distance? Could the accident have saved me somehow?

I shoved one of the bottles deep under the seat, then reclaimed my crutches and the second bottle for the awkward journey back up the driveway.

I stood in the kitchen for a moment staring at the bottle. The negotiations were short. I didn't know if I was going to the cabin to dry out or to drink myself to death. But now, the circumstances had changed. *I need this now. I've been abandoned by everyone. I am alone. Why does their drinking get to be normal? I'm normal; my drinking has just manifested in a string of inopportune luck. Look at all the success I've achieved. Look at my house, Nathan's grades, my car, my credit score. They don't get to tell me I have a problem. I don't have a problem… Just bad luck.*

I cracked the cap, gazing across the kitchen at a glass that was too far away. I awkwardly tipped the bottle back with my left hand, mocking the brace on my right, imbibing the first of many drinks I would have during my injury rehabilitation.

...repetitive and compulsive use, despite negative consequences.

The next five months looked identical to the few months prior to my accident. I drank day and night, never to belligerence, but to a medicated state that kept my brain and pain sufficiently dull. Due to my injuries, I had abandoned my years-long practice of walking in to get Nathan from school. Instead, I got in line with the other parents in the curbside carpool line. Carpool had its own degree of chaos surrounding it, but if I arrived about 20 minutes early, I could guarantee a predictable pull up spot where Nathan would know to look for me.

On an early May day, four months past my accident, I pulled into carpool, per usual. I threw my vehicle in park and took a brief nap. Not hearing the cars fire up to proceed to the front curb of the school, a mom knocked on my window and asked if I was all right.

Startled, I straightened up and said, "Yes, of course. Just fell asleep." I proceeded a little too rapidly to catch up with my place in line, rubbing the curb as I settled into my spot.

Maybe it was the smell of my breath, or the rubbing of the curb, or my bloodshot eyes. Any one of these was sufficient reason for the flashing lights of police officers to surround me and pin in my car.

What a reversal. What a removal from a place of reverence. Parents at my son's charter school walking in, kids hearing the school bell and walking out, and me on full display in front of everyone doing a sobriety check, on crutches in the middle of it all. And somehow, my countenance broke to a state where it didn't even matter. My family and closest friends had already passed judgment on me. Why not add the communal collective to the masses who would easily diagnose what I refused to acknowledge within myself?

There is a saying, that there is not a single problem that alcohol can't make worse. It's a saying because it is true. I had found a new low. After failing the sobriety check in my son's school parking lot, the police zip tied my wrists and took me to jail.

◦ ̋F ₿ €̋ ◦

Tammy and I eased past the Florence Supermax Penitentiary. The fence sparkled in a way that suggested it was fairly new. We read the large sign of the entry and looked through the guard station.

We quietly picked up speed as the county highway led us back to more formulary, mountain scenery.

Tammy asked, "How long until we get to the castle?" A long pause. "Jeff? Jeff, what are you thinking about, love?"

"I'm thinking there has to be a fine line, but a big difference, between prison sex and dungeon sex. One seems forced, but the other seems suggestive."

Tammy looked for permission to smile, and then just shook her head and laughed.

"Well? I mean, it sounds the same, but doesn't dungeon sex seem friendlier? Like, a mutual planning took place?"

"I thought you were thinking about something deep." Tammy kept laughing. "You had an intense stare."

"I was, I guess. I was thinking about being in jail... I've come a long way." I looked at Tammy for some validation.

"Yes, we sure have."

Chapter 5

The Mountain Road

1:15 PM

We were clearly tourists, winding on an unfamiliar mountain road working its way into the expanse of the San Isabel National Forest, which required a tad more caution than if we knew where we were going. It might have been all well and good, taking our time a few miles under the speed limit so as to absorb the beauty of the mountains and early fall foliage starting to turn, but the cars that were in a hurry behind us stole our contentedness in being casual travelers. The single-lane road boasted exceptional elevation gains and hairpin turns, but regardless of the danger, vehicles followed at a close distance behind us and moved to the center line to view their passing options. They were sending me nonverbal signals that I was not going fast enough.

"I'm gonna pull over and let them pass," I said, warning Tammy that I'd be heading off the road in the direction of 150-foot pine trees, so she wouldn't think I had lost control.

We allowed the three-car build-up behind us to pass, forgiving their appearance of rudeness. Even though many areas of Colorado mountain highways might have caution signs as low as 15 miles per hour on a blind corner, it is always relative to the driver and their familiarity with the road.

It was a driving behavior we knew well, and one we were on the other side of not long ago. Prior to buying our new home last year, Tammy and I decided to live up at our own mountain cabin. The road up there was similar, so I recognized the annoyance of the folks behind me as my own, and graciously moved to the side.

Thoughts of our cabin flush me with the most defining moments of my life. The 875-square-foot raised ranch home, adorned with thick, wavy alpine siding, was neatly tucked between two hillsides. A gentle, meandering creek split the difference of each mountainside, flowing next to the cabin, trickling with the sound of serenity. It is where Tammy and I hosted a small family gathering for our wedding prior to moving there, and eventually, it is where I would turn the corner and start considering that my wrestling with alcohol was not with external circumstances. I began to admit that the battle might have lay within.

Before our cabin provided the setting of future hope and the potential of freedom, first it opened itself as a refuge in my darkest hours.

◦"F ฿ €"◦

You don't drive your vehicle into a school parking lot, knowingly under the influence of alcohol, and then get to blame the system. This is who you are, a citizen newly released from jail, a court date to be determined later, an embattled monster. A wobbling contradiction of a person who knows the right thing to do but has succumbed time and time again to choosing alcohol instead.

In a way, I felt like the opposite of Will in *Good Will Hunting*. Will, the character played by Matt Damon, started as a janitor and ended up recognizing his genius. I started as a genetic researcher with a publishable discovery at age 21, and was now a drunken janitor about to receive his second DUI at age 36. My trajectory was not heading towards elevation, but towards descent.

The new DUI impressed enough fear to shake me sober for a few weeks. The internal shame combined with the external public pressure begged me to evaluate whether being addicted to alcohol is who I truly was. How could this be? I had achieved all the external measures of success. I had crafted a whole decade of my adult life where alcohol was a complete non-issue.

I shuddered as I evaluated a whole other set of paralyzing consequences. My entire friend and family structure drank. The risk of giving in and admitting defeat carried the risk of losing my whole tribe. As I observed how they seemed perfectly fine to recognize that I had a problem and distance their drinking from me, this suggested that being able to drink was intricately linked with maintaining my friendships. It wasn't as if they said, "Hey Jeff, we value you as a friend. Let's just keep hanging out, but we'll do it a different way, without alcohol." Nope. In their absence, they might as well have said, "Hey man, sorry, we love you, but we love booze more. Good luck."

So good luck, it was. I was on my own.

Friday happy hour would approach, and I wouldn't receive a call or text. The silence from my neighbors, who I had previously opened my home to on a weekly basis, was them trying to do me a favor, trying to protect me from myself. The evening would unfold, lonely. It was only later that I would see a broadcast on social media displaying a great time being shared by everyone but me.

There is a certain amount of lag time between getting arrested for drinking and driving, and experiencing the consequences. In my case, my consequences were projected to start kicking in on July 5th with a DMV hearing. I would lose my driver's license for a year and then have a breathalyzer linked to my car for an additional year after that. The criminal consequences would be determined later, but would undoubtedly involve jail time. Until July 5th, I was free, deemed innocent by our system.

Staring at the logistical consequences of a second DUI was overwhelming. In combination with still recovering from the car accident four months prior, I was the single dad of an 11-year-old, living in an affluent suburb of Denver. I would have to try and run a business, where I travel to multiple locations nightly, without a license. Bills for attorneys, fines, and therapy classes would pinch an already strained financial situation. My fear and anxiety were reaching an apex.

A formal commitment that I had made before all of this had happened was looming around the Memorial Day weekend. I had been asked to be the officiant for my friends' wedding. The couple, Jen and Leo, were a degree of separation from my inner circle, living way on the north side of Denver. Jen and I had been attending the same social gatherings since my early twenties, and I was thrilled that she had finally met someone as bright and charming as Leo.

The ceremony would take place on Saturday; I started writing and preparing it on Thursday. This was not something that I did often. In fact, I had only attempted it once before, delivering a lovely service. I worked backwards into my computer files to find some of my notes from that previous ceremony. It struck me as I identified the date that those notes were prepared around the time of Mindy's infidelity. I felt a sting. *Had I been standing up there delivering that service while Mindy was in the crowd burying the knowledge of her indiscretion? Had she even cheated yet? Would it have been worse if she'd done it after I joined that young couple with the words I had spoken?*

I had done a pretty good job of inadvertently staying sober after the school parking lot arrest, but there I was, sitting with all of these dreadful feelings of betrayal and injustice while trying to formulate the wording of faithfulness and commitment. I couldn't handle the feelings, the lack of belief in the promises of love, and the unrelenting memory of promises broken. I took my first drink that Thursday night, convincing myself that it would calm my nerves and soften my heart.

Trying to remove feelings and escape anxiety through alcohol never works. Even if they are quelled for a short time, it's as if the feelings are harvested, incubated, and then return exponentially. One drink turned into many, and by the time the sun broke into the neighborhood on the Saturday morning of the wedding, I stared at a blank sheet of paper, with a heart that read just as empty.

Too intoxicated to perform at the wedding, a slobbering mess, I sat in a lawn chair that faced my car in the closed garage. Undoubtedly, I had unearthed a new low, being someone who internally professed to value the care of others, now laid to waste by alcohol, disappointing friends and a crowd of people on their most important day.

The hypocrisy of who I had become was unbearable, and for a solid moment, I considered turning on the car in that closed garage, removing the pain permanently. I wanted desperately to escape this pathetic contradiction that couldn't be reconciled.

With my face swollen from crying and my chest heaving like a pinned-down animal, I called my dad, whimpering, begging him to come pick me up. I needed to get away. *I needed help.*

I come from an incredibly loving family. I grew up lower-middle class, with two active, attentive, hard-working parents. We weren't abused, and alcohol use was infrequent and moderate. If my upbringing lacked for anything, it was communication. Any affirmative, or even instructive, language from my family was minimal. They lived by example, by doing, by showing the way, always generous with their time and acts, and not really talking about why. I took away those values as virtues, viewing productivity and acts of service as the highest form of showing love.

As adults, those values work both ways. It never occurred to my parents, always the givers, that they could become a burden on me; likewise, I never conceived of putting a strain on them. To call my father to help me in a time of crisis was almost like breaking some unwritten code, a silent vow that we never really wanted to be the standard.

My dad picked me up, his 36-year-old boy limping out of his three-car garage. I climbed into his work truck, picking up my right leg to swing it into the cab, still not having its own strength from the femur break five months ago.

His chin quivering, he eked out, "Where are we going?"

As if a whisper might deaden the slur, I said, "The cabin."

My instinct was to protect him from how ugly this might be, so almost immediately, I asked him to pull into a gas station with a split liquor store attached. The unfamiliarity of any of this was off the charts for my dad, so he did, thankfully, without question. I lumbered into the gas station side, crossed into the open threshold that housed the liquor, and bought a pack of cigarettes and two mini bottles of vodka. Putting them into my pocket, I returned to the truck and we were on our way.

We took the 13-mile winding road west. Throughout the journey I silently stared out my passenger-side window, watching the elevated pine trees cast shadows onto the creek. In open spaces the sun pierced the water, making it sparkling and vibrant. Large rock outcroppings forced tight hairpin turns, but even with all the movement of the truck, I sat frozen, catatonic, not knowing how I could possibly explain to my father the state to which I had been reduced.

We reached the cabin and I sat out on the south-facing deck to get some sun. My dad came out to silently sit with me. Still a "closet smoker" in front of my dad after all these years, I did something that would set the tone of our weekend: I lit a cigarette in front of him. *No secrets.*

I don't remember the exact words used, but there were a lot of them. I told him everything about the divorce, everything I had buried in my attempt to maintain a co-parenting friendship with Mindy. Even two years after the divorce, I still protected her by never revealing her infidelity as the definitive reason for our separation. I coldly spilled those truths to him in that moment.

My dad and I didn't devise any resolutions. We didn't speak of a plan of action. He merely let me get it out. He listened and allowed me to graffiti the blank chalkboard, scratching out a complex equation of all I had been holding in. The crisp mountain air tried to rinse over our current moment with honesty, but I polluted it with blame. I blamed Mindy's cheating. I relayed the downstream effects of my parents being emotionally detached. I articulated how my mom could have been more unconditionally supportive of our marriage. I sided against my sister's and friends' choice to leave me in isolation. I had called my dad for help, but I didn't need help with alcohol; I needed to self-edit my selective excuses as to why alcohol had been the answer.

Our midday conversation strayed into the late afternoon. Having run out of words and tears, Dad and I settled into the family room of the cabin. We turned on *Cheers* and watched it from the pilot episode. I imagined that he sat watching the TV, fretting only about the external world and this problem that couldn't be solved in a tidy 30-minute episode, while I sat trying to immerse myself in the story, trying to escape my own.

My dad dozed off, allowing me the opportunity to head out to the front tiled patio and have a cigarette. Noticing my hands starting to shake, I took a quarter nip of the one-ounce vodka shot in my pocket, minimizing the possibility of a full crash or a seizure. It was one thing to have unloaded such a verbal and mental barrage upon my father, but I couldn't have forgiven myself if I'd let him see the full physical spectrum of alcohol withdrawal.

That first night, I'd excuse myself, telling my dad I couldn't sleep and that I wanted to be by the cigarettes. The late evening chill drifting through the single-pane windows could not account for the degree to which my hand was shaking, trying to take a controlled grip of my lighter. I sat still, looking out into the dark expanse, replaying the words of the nurse six months earlier, *"We already knew what the problem was. You're a drunk."*

My eyelids became heavy, teasing me that I might get a reprieve, begging me to go inside and seek more comfortable quarters. I resisted, knowing I did not deserve comfort. I imagined a backyard full of joyous celebrants' faces turning cold as they heard of my abandonment. I slithered from my chair to the cold patio tile, warming myself into a ball. Sweating. Shaking. Seeing the presumptive disappointments on Jen's and Leo's faces. I closed my eyes, knowing that if I could ride this out, then tomorrow would come, although I wasn't entirely sure that I wanted it to.

Sunday had arrived, and although we had well into Monday on the Memorial Day weekend to do whatever it was that we were doing, I told my dad I was ready to go home on Sunday afternoon. I had spent the better part of Saturday trying to relay the pain of my relational history, supplemented with the obvious state of my condition. All of the words that I had mustered gave way to conversation fatigue and shame. My display had been put forth, and we had both played out our parts: he providing unconditional support and availability, and me purging dishonesty and alcohol. Any clear revelations of the next step to take beyond that, eluded us both.

We traveled back down that tight forest road. My same stoic glare out the window met the mountain landscape with befuddled confusion. How can a world that is so beautiful, be so dark? How could I prop myself up as being good, when the reality was me making decisions this bad?

My mental acuity was foggy, but I had patches of clearing that reminded me of all the consequences of alcohol abuse that were waiting for me at the bottom of that mountain. On July 5th, the system would put me in a stranglehold, debilitating how I normally maintained an already busy and complicated life. I had now added into the turmoil the destruction of a wedding and relationships, letting down so many people who I truly cared about.

As the final stretch of the mountain road offered its last turn, 50-foot rocky canyon walls opened like a mouth into a meadow that led me back to my suburb. My dad asked, "You feeling okay?"

"No, I'm not." With all of the same emphatic honesty I had delivered over the past 24 hours, I said softly, "I feel like such a piece of shit." Never unsettling my gaze forward, a tear dropped off my cheek.

□″F ℬ ℭ″□

With the eager cars passing, Tammy and I eased our way back onto the narrow highway and achieved a safe and comfortable speed. The surrounding mountain landscape showed hints of fall amongst the tall Austrian and Blue Spruce pines. The sunrays slid sideways and lit up pockets of Aspen trees starting to boast a bright yellow, and reddish-purple patches of Scrub Oak dotted the landscape.

It's an understatement in recovery, the degree to which you need to be fully present. An addict pushes forward so hard through present time to make it to the part of the day where they can change their thoughts and close down their brain. Even now, there is serenity in not going full throttle to get somewhere else, not being pushed by the expectations of people behind me, but to be perfectly comfortable in the moment. It's a serenity that doesn't have you constantly mentally wavering between doing the good now, versus applying "the fix" later. You are where you are supposed to be in the moment. There is a center, a place where mental rest is, and you are not outside looking for it. You are in it.

The torturous cognitive dissonance is gone.

We reached the plateau of the first section of forest and started heading back down the western side of the mountain. Winding down briefly, it opened to wide valley displaying grand pastures, running horses, and a rustic, crooked split-rail fence. A classic red barn's color jumped out against the towering grey Sangre de Christo mountain range that revealed itself another 50 miles in the backdrop.

If I could have safely removed my eyes from the road long enough, I would have looked at Tammy.

I would've stared at her and contrasted that horrible day where I couldn't look towards my father. I would remember that day driving back with him into the abyss as being my lowest, my most confused, and my most terrified self, not knowing how I would ever bring myself through the chaos I had created. How would I ever make my way through this mess?

If I could've, I would've looked at Tammy.

Jeff Bowersox

Chapter 6

The Fork

1:35 PM

Dropping down through our first large mountain range, our Jeep slowly approached a fork in the highway, which had me quickly trying to recall the map I had studied earlier that morning. I pursed my lips, not saying what I was thinking. I'd thought I had a strong sense of the area, but once you're out in the expanse and unfamiliar with how far you've traveled, it opens everything up to a little guess work.

"Do me a favor, love?" I asked casually. "On your phone, google Bishop Castle, so we can punch it into the navigation?"

Tammy, phone in hand, returned serve with a slight smile on her face. "Sorry, no service."

Hmmm. "I'm pretty sure it was more south than west. I guess we have a fifty-fifty chance of being right?"

"Which is an optimistic way of saying *you* have a fifty-fifty chance of getting us lost?" Tammy teased, her smile expanding to a giggle.

I'm not actually worried about making the wrong turn, about fearing any blowback from Tammy; she genuinely couldn't be any cooler in that respect. Us getting time together and doing something different encompassed our goal today, and in that way, we'd already reached our destination.

I often brag about how crazy I am about her. There is one word I use to describe Tammy, and it is a small word that we dissected at its first use as quite possibly being an insult; she is *easy*. It's not a trivial thing to say. In a playful way, I've had fun with the phrase, "You're *easy*," relating it to sexual suggestions, watching a garbage action movie, or her wanting dishwashing towels for Christmas. I can't express enough, though, how *easy* she was in all of the important areas where life was *hard*. She encapsulated love, grace, compassion, and kindness, all wrapped up into that profound four-letter word.

I took an unconfident left, thinking about how getting lost might just add to our adventure, and knowing that I'd never be as lost as that Fourth of July day when Tammy and I first met.

□˝F ℬ €˝□

Roughly a month had passed since my suicidal breakdown when I called my dad to come rescue me. Although it had been a serious moment, I didn't let it command the type of follow through it deserved. I didn't design a plan, and I never even considered that to resolve the consequences of my drinking, I had to first tackle alcohol itself. I arranged some token gestures that would help improve my chances in court for the DUI. I submitted myself to voluntary urine tests when I knew I was clean, and I obtained my first ever therapist, who I thought I could use for a drafted letter showing my level of contrition to the courts.

June became July, and while my drinking continued intermittently, I still tried to brandish the bottle with the same summer normalcy as everyone else.

July 4th had arrived with a tad more irony that year: a day recognizing freedom and independence, leading into July 5th when I would lose my driver's license for one year, followed by jail time, puncturing any grandiose idea that I would *actually be free*.

A tradition since I was a small boy, my last day of driving led me to a Fourth of July celebration at my uncle's ranch on an outstretched piece of land about 40 miles north of Denver. The barbeque checked all of the boxes of a picturesque redneck gathering: hundreds of blue-collar workers and their families, wearing farmer's tans that exposed poorly thought out, aging tattoos. Glorious smells of chicken wings butted in the air against bad country music. People roamed the grounds catching up, their one time of year trying to remember the names of the folks they'd seen every year prior. The ranch boasted large barns and outbuildings that dwarfed the house itself, and people were always keenly aware that outside of the barn, beside the vintage avocado fridge-turned-kegerator, is where the party really started.

I didn't have any reservations about drinking that day. Everybody drinks on the Fourth. I was of course cognizant that my closest family, the people who knew what I had been through over the last six months, were there. For them, seeing me with a drink must have looked like a 65-year-old who had undergone a tracheotomy shoving a cigarette through the hole in his neck. I didn't care what they thought. I just wanted to be like everyone else.

After depositing my homemade mushroom salsa on the plastic banquet table and working through the exchange of pleasantries, I settled in with a beer and a game of horseshoes in the far corner of the property. Playing well in the horseshoes tournament positioned you at the pinnacle of the social hierarchy in this environment, and while I can self-profess to be more of the effeminate, non-redneck variety, I loved winning at horseshoes. My matches were going well, and while I stood against the chain-link fence, waiting for others to take their turns playing, I saw her… Tammy.

Striding in from the makeshift dirt parking lot at least a hundred yards away, she was hard to miss. I gazed across the lawn and watched her walk towards the festivities. She was tall and lean, well over six-foot. Her pink tank top beat back all of the muted colors of people wearing cut-off jean shorts and over-worn Harley Davidson T-shirts. She was clearly with someone, equally as tall, but that did not deflate the intrigue of watching her from a distance.

I spent most of the afternoon into the evening in that far quadrant of the yard. We were having a blast, as my horseshoes partner and I were taking down each new competitor, eliminating them from the bracket. Dusk started giving way and we had won the tournament, so we made our way back to the front of the barn to revel in our earned glory. People gathered around the large concrete slab driveway adjoining the barn for an illegal and industrious homemade fireworks display.

My brother-in-law, Danny, approached me with a coy look on his face. He popped his eyes to another level of open, signaling to me that I better pay attention. "Hey, I think you really need to meet somebody. This is Tammy."

Danny had discovered that the man she'd walked in with was her son. At a closer viewing, Tammy appeared more in my age bracket, still perfectly put together.

"Hi, I'm Jeff. So... *You've* never been here before." I trusted my data back-up of never having seen anyone like her, period, let alone at our countryside gathering.

"No, I haven't. I came with my son. He works for Marvin," she said, smiling. "They told me I have to get out."

"Do you want to sit?" I gestured towards the wooden picnic table and bench.

We sat on the table, feet on the bench, looking towards the bustle of amateur pyros jockeying for which fireworks they were going to light.

"How do you know Marvin?" she asked.

"He's my uncle. I've been coming to this thing for 30-plus years."

"So, you know everybody?"

"Well, mostly. I mean, I see the same people year after year, but I have a hard time recalling their names, let alone knowing them."

"Like, who's that over there?" She pointed.

"That's Bennie. He wears the same button-down shirt with American flags and chicken drumettes on it every year. I think it's his way of saying, 'I'll be in charge of whether the wings *do or do not* give you *salmonella* poisoning.' I guarantee his big face wasn't that red when he got here. This might be the only day he gets sun all year."

"He seems happy." She paused. "You seem happy. You're not here with anyone?"

"Of course, I'm happy. I beat these hillbillies at their own game with a teenage girl as my partner. How could I not be happy?" I smiled. "My son, Nathan. He's over there. I'm with him. Other than that, no, I'm not together with anyone, if that's what you mean."

Tammy gave subtle inferences that she had noticed me, as I had noticed her. She added, "I was watching you playing and smiling. I thought, he must be married."

This sprung us into a night of conversation. We talked about our kids, our former marriages, our jobs. It was comfortable. *Really* comfortable. The noise level of the fireworks and crowd gave us reason to be close, and if I needed to lean towards her ear to clarify conversation, I'd settle my nose behind her ear just long enough to let her know I was relishing her presence.

The fireworks launched overhead, growing bigger with the gathering of people matching their intensity, until a final clapping of hands signaled their end. I felt a jolt of panic at the reality that meeting someone this lovely at a moment of my life burdened with such ugliness was a non-starter. The smolder of the lingering air matched my spirit, so alive and bright a few moments before, but now thinned to gray.

Tammy's son and his two friends approached us. They carried the jovial disposition of a final out in a baseball game, a look that said, "That was fun, but it's time to move on."

I made small talk with her son, asking if he enjoyed working with my uncle. The conversation elicited genuine interest, but quickly moved to him gesturing that they should get going. "I think my ride is ready to head out."

"Yeah." I brushed the backside of my index finger softly back and forth on the outer side of her leg. "I wish you could stay a while longer."

"Me too." She seemed sincere. "I came with them, though. I have no idea where I am."

Almost understanding that my future predicament shouldn't belabor us parting, I said, resigned, "I understand. It was amazing meeting you. You made this the best night, Tammy. You have no idea."

"It was great meeting you too, Jeff." Smiling, she scooched herself from the table top, and used those long legs to stride towards her group, trying to catch up.

I sat there, elated and saddened all at the same time. I'd be delusional to think I could offer value to a future relationship. My fairytale fireworks were easily doused by my oncoming DUI penalties the following day. I looked down at the charred concrete, shaking my head, pouring self-judgment on my own stupidity.

I felt a tug on the back of my shirt. Shaken out of my condemnation, a guy had run back from the car that Tammy was getting into. Giving me a slip of paper, he said, "Dude, you're really bad at this."

"I'm sorry?"

"This is her number. Tammy's number."

"Oh," I said, my surprise and complete ineptitude being proven. "Err. Yes, tell her thanks."

Waiting, almost laughing, he said, "Now it's your turn. Would *you* like *her* to have *your* number?"

"Oh…. Yeah. Yes!"

As if he knew that I was hopelessly ill prepared, he handed me a pen and a piece of paper.

Getting her number didn't make me feel any better. As I stared at the clutter of the spent fireworks on the ground, I felt more like the person in the office who hadn't gone in with the coworkers on the winning lotto ticket. They let you look at it and even hold the ticket, but you wouldn't be collecting the winnings. I slipped her number into my wallet and headed to my sister's RV to sleep, more aware of my future loneliness than ever. Tomorrow, the DMV would suspend my driver's license. I had a lot to figure out beyond navigating a frivolous relationship.

A week had passed since the Fourth of July. As expected, I had received a phone call from my attorney dictating that the hearing with the DMV had ruled in favor of the authorities. Settled into that reality, Nathan and I were throwing the baseball back and forth in our cul-de-sac. It was one of my favorite things to do, the methodical catching and releasing of the ball, timed with intermittent conversation with my son… My cell phone rang.

"Hello? Yeah. Hey! No, of course I do… It was such a fun night. No, I just… It's been a little complicated around here. Listen, I'm having a game of catch with my son. Is it okay if I give you a call later tonight? Okay… Sure thing. Bye."

"Who was that?" Nathan sensed my hesitation.

"Remember Tower Barbie… from the Fourth of July?"

"*Yeeeeees.* You gonna call her back?"

"I don't *knooooooow,*" I matched his tone, snapping the ball back in his direction.

That same evening, my therapist paid me a visit. We had scheduled the appointment at my home, since she knew that I was unable to drive to her office. As we worked through our hour, I mentioned that I had met someone. After doting over Tammy's appearance and how easily we had connected, I launched into multiple areas of deflection as to why I shouldn't pursue it. *I would come off as such a loser… I don't have a license… I'll be going to jail… Business is going to be complicated and absorb my time… Nathan doesn't need this variable… I'll be financially pinched…*

She studied me for a moment. "Jeff, do you realize how many ways you just told me you don't deserve to be loved?"

"Yeah, I guess."

"Do you think you deserve happiness?"

"Honestly, I don't know." I sat questioning how I've let all of my drinking consequences pile on shame. Maybe I was punishing myself more than any authority ever could. It might not have even been the shame. Protecting and presenting a well-maintained life, a false identity at this point, remained my default "go to." Isolation seemed safer to my ego than showing anyone the holes in my armor.

"You deserve love and happiness. We all do. If you like her and think she'll bring meaning and joy, you pursue meaning and joy. A life full of purpose and meaning is the antidote for substance abuse. You build the life you don't want to run or escape from. You call her, and be honest with what you are going through. *Be vulnerable*," she said, breaking through my uncertainty.

I called Tammy that evening. It took less than a minute for us to pick up where we'd left off, affirming our connection, and shortly after, I started relaying why I'd hesitated in calling her since the Fourth of July. There is no way to be self-protective in such moments, no way to make a DUI in your son's school parking lot look attractive; the data was the data.

Being vulnerable is taking off the protective sheen of who you'd like to be, and instead, allowing someone to see you as you are, blemishes and all. After letting her know I'd love to see her again, but was incapable of driving, we arranged a Friday happy hour at my sister's community pool.

That Friday arrived with all of the same eagerness of a preteen meeting a group of friends at the playground where first experimental kisses would be exchanged. An anxious buzzing in my belly stirred as I watched her park at the quaint pool, her Saab SUV fitting right in with the surrounding McMansions that littered the horizon. Watching her get out of the car sparked my senses, identical to the way I had felt a couple of weeks earlier, but now, dressed in a business casual pantsuit that framed her perfection, she gave off a sexy, sophisticated vibe that hadn't come across at the barbeque. *What was I doing? Who did I think I was, trying to pull this off?*

We exchanged hugs in the parking lot as I directed her to the pool's clubhouse, where she could change. Our night, and into the early morning, engulfed us with the same comfortable conversation sparked by the night we met. Poolside, we chatted; our virtues and life goals were similar, our pasts peppered with undertones of disappointments and betrayal, and our desire for leisure and relief were in sync.

Friday bled into Saturday where we took Nathan to the Renaissance Festival. We walked along the grounds as Nathan sped up to the rock-climbing feature. I linked my finger with hers, wondering if she felt silly being with someone shorter than her. What a relief, to have my largest concerns of alcohol be downgraded, to move on to basic human insecurities.

The Renaissance Festival ended, and we landed back at my house, continuing our marathon date. After making dinner, we continued talking, drinking, and laughing well into the evening on my back porch.

In some mystical way, it didn't have to be said. We were already together. It may have been that I was emboldened with Tammy being debriefed about my worst mistakes. My excess drinking had landed me in a place of immobility and future strain, but sitting on the back porch, I felt moved to test this "vulnerability thing" further. Up until this point, it had been a relief to lay myself open and bare. I was flawed, yet she still made me feel like I was good enough.

I broke into a more serious tone. "So, I'm not like, a porn guy, per se. Like, I'm uncomfortable with the fact that I view it at all, but if you were to comb my computer, you would see retro, like, the occasional '70s and '80s porn movies in my history."

Silence... She studied me for a second, not sure how to respond. "Well, I... *What?*"

I continued, trying to salvage my honesty with some humor, "So, I feel like current porn could be exploitative and damaging to people, but the stuff that's 30 to 40 years old... well, what's done is done." I looked for any signs that she would be revolted and walk out. I continued, "I guess I just wanted to warn you, you know, about all the hair. Girls with teased up hair, Aqua Net, mullets, bad moustaches, and I mean, the butt hair at times can be a little unsight—"

She kissed me. She grabbed the back of my head and pulled me to her face as hard as we would ever kiss.

My forehead met hers. I was relieved. "I guess what I'm really saying is that I'm tired of being guarded. I'm tired of trying to be perfect all the time. Of hiding. Of secrets. They haven't served me. It's exhausting... and I don't want to hide anything from you."

That's it. I hit the reset button. Pre-July 4th, my internal computer had given me the blue screen of death: car accident, six broken bones, shameful DUI, unreliable minister of a wedding, and suicidal thoughts. On July 4th, I had miraculously rebooted, met Tammy, laid my life open and bare, and begun trudging through the swampy, stinky mess I had created.

But it didn't stink. In between contracts in the telecom field, Tammy wanted to use her downtime to learn more about my business. We'd go out at night, her driving, and service and manage my accounts. In my adult life, I'd been the doer of all things, but where I lacked, Tammy added thoughts of how to manage and promote. It was revelatory, and long past due, actually partnering with someone. We performed work together with a strong report, and afterwards, stopped at the 24-hour gym, late at night, having it all to ourselves. My strength and dexterity, depleted from the accident six months ago, started to return, not just putting a bounce in my step, but a bounce in my heart.

My drinking turned back to *normal* insomuch that it was regulated by court-ordered, random tests. Tammy never had to witness my former drunken despair, only the view of moderate drinking that the system monitored on my behalf.

Surprisingly, where the consequences of my DUI were supposed to be loathed, I acquired solid introspection and tools that I would try to apply to moderate drinking going forward. I started attending court-ordered group therapy classes. At one point when I was sitting in class, my phone rang. It was Mindy. I'm not certain if it was the look on my face or my caretaking predisposition, but my counselor gave me an empathetic nod to step out and take the call. Mindy was calling to ask for more money. She understood, and said as much, that our agreement remained fair, but that her Lupus was causing her complications and any contribution would be understood as charity and not something that I had to do. I was paralyzed. The turmoil of indecision had left me short of breath...

My counselor walked out. "You okay?"

"Yeah, I mean, I don't know. My ex is having health problems and is asking if I can contribute to her financial costs," I responded, perplexed.

"Jeff... *Jeff!*" He raised his voice and pointed to his building. "Look where you are... *Looooook!* At what point are you going to stop always taking care of other people and start taking care of yourself?"

I was jolted by the revelation, a micro-reality of a bigger problem. "Of course. Yeah." I mean, that was my answer in this moment, but that *was the answer!* Enabling others, putting their weight on my back had always driven me to a certain place of success and stroked my ego, but it left nothing in my own tank. I had outperformed everyone in my former laboratory, turned around and pastored our community, and then doubled our income by being a janitor at night, all while attending to Nathan's and Mindy's needs. When it came to my own personal care, I would use alcohol for the quickest, most efficient way to adjust my mood or to turn off a day's worth of responsibilities. Moments like this were illuminative, and they came in lockstep with having a clearer head in the forced absence of alcohol. Counter to my programmed impulse, I rejected Mindy's request for assistance.

Weaving their way into the first few months of Tammy's and my relationship were my DUI court proceedings. A 45-day jail sentence loomed. The month prior, we had organized my business to be fully staffed, even though technically, the jail was a work release program. I designed my release itinerary such that, since I worked from home, they released me during my work hours to my "home office" from 2 PM to midnight. I was there when Nathan returned from school, so we'd make dinner together, watch an evening of Netflix, and then Nathan would go to bed. Later, Tammy and I hung out until it was time for me to head back to jail from midnight to 2 PM the next day. In jail, I ordered all the classic books from Amazon that life full of missed Jeopardy trivia reminded me I should have read, along with copious varieties of chocolate with commissary money. My jail time was spent reading and relaxing, a balance that had escaped me when I was "free."

I'd wake up and have breakfast with the other inmates, getting to know their stories. Ninety percent of them were in what was called the Multiple Offenders Program, meaning that they had three drug or alcohol offenses, tying them to the jail system for a full year. I thought to myself, "Man, how could you go through this process once and then screw up and return. *Not for me*."

Overall, I learned a few things. Jail was a pain in the ass, and at every turn you felt less than human and embarrassed about your conduct from the authorities. But I also learned that, prior to jail, I had never really prioritized my own personal well-being. I learned that I liked jail, and was able to pinpoint my issues with carving out time for real rest. Second, since I had removed myself from my science colleagues, and my neighborhood friends had continued to isolate their drinking from me, I also learned that I craved community. My group therapy friends, and now my jail inmates, stoked comradery and banter that had been lacking.

Overall, I had "soldiered up" and made it through the worst of my circumstances, cultivating a brilliant and loving new relationship with Tammy where she never made me feel less than I had already felt of myself. Exiting jail on the last day, I was fit with an alcohol monitor on my leg, a bulky electronic recording device that tracked any alcohol in my blood stream. Tammy and I were intimate that evening, and although having this clunky device on my leg made me feel like such a loser, she playfully teased, "Oh, this is so awesome! It's like making out with Robo-Cop!"

Whenever the sting of former mistakes lured me into shame, Tammy picked me up with grace.

Alcohol played a minimal role in our fledgling courtship. The county's probation system had a rigid schedule of checks and balances, forcing me sober. It imbued a false security, like I didn't have a drinking problem; when required to, I stopped. There were, however, moments when I figured out the alcohol testing schedule, and on those nights, we casually drank. There was always a slight thrill in that... *I'm still an adult. Look at all I take care of and achieve. You can't keep me in detention forever.* And although I convinced myself that I was an adult, sneaking around the system, it looked more like me passing a note across the classroom when the teacher wasn't looking.

We spent one hundred percent of our time together. As the months flew by, we seemed to cross the threshold of any imaginary boundary that might have warned us that our synergy was only real because it was new. But it wasn't just early passions. We enjoyed the true companionship that filled every measure of our time. My hours and preoccupations, once filled with alcohol, self-pity, and destruction, were now filled with a future that looked whole, a future that I still wasn't certain that I deserved, but one that I embraced with gratitude.

On December 30th, I slipped away to a job with an employee of mine. While the employee wrapped up a final construction clean that we were doing, I paced in front of an adjacent jewelry store, a pace that still carried a slight limp from the car accident exactly one year ago to the day. I squatted down in the courtyard adjoining the jewelry store, as if getting closer to the holy ground I was about to tread on would add to the contrition. The sharp pain in my hip almost reminded me of my unworthiness. For the first time since before my divorce, I prayed. "God, please. I... I know I don't deserve this, and I haven't made decisions that should curry any favor, but if you could shine your light on me. If... I guess, if you could please lead the way?"

As deeply in my spirit as I could witness, I heard, "I already have."

As my thoughts flooded with Tammy striding into our Fourth of July barbeque, my soul filled. "Yeah," I whispered, "you have."

I walked in to buy her ring.

As January 1st put the former year to rest, the juxtaposition of the lowest of lows and the highest of highs could not be oversold. It would be that day, the start of our new year, that Tammy would excitedly say, "Yes! Yes! Yes!" when I asked her to marry me. I had learned enough about Tammy over the past six months to know that we would be wonderful together going forward. What I hadn't learned was her frightened aversion to cliffside marriage proposals, so her "Yes! Yes! Yes!" was more of a shouting from the distance because she would not come out and meet me on the ledge.

Our first day of the new year ended with our resolve to combine our futures. That night, we nestled on the sofa, Tammy perching her head on my chest. I drew my finger down the length of her gently sloped nose. I touched my knuckle to her cheekbone. In the serenity of our moment, I said, "You know, we should probably have our wedding on the Fourth of July?"

"Ohhh, I like it. That would be perfect, wouldn't it?"

"The thing is… I'm the reigning horseshoes champion, so… we might have to take our wedding reception to Uncle Marvin's barbeque?"

"Sounds perfect still," she said.

And for the first time, I kissed the top of her head and honored her with the compliment, *"You're easy."*

Chapter 7

The Warning Signs

<u>2:00 PM</u>

Winding turns and mountainous passes stretched us into Southern Colorado for another twenty minutes. Sounds of alt-folk music from the speakers meshed perfectly with the wilderness and sparse human habitation. Still not entirely sure if I was heading in the right direction, signs of life appeared around a bend where someone's vehicle was pulled over onto the shoulder. I slowed cautiously, seeing another car beyond the first.

"Hey, this might be it!"

Sure enough, a random single-lane highway in the middle of the San Isabel National Forest sprouted signs of life all over. People on the opposite side of the road were tucked into uninviting crevices, a few angled with their car heading up an embankment. Some folks stood, camera in hand, ready to dart across.

Obviously, the tighter the mishmash of cars, the closer to our entry point we must be. Trying to be cautious of the foot traffic, I searched for a first glimpse of this piece of internet folklore. Then a beat-up, '70s flatbed pickup with makeshift rails boasting large hand-painted letters presented itself:

BISHOP CASTLE

Passing the entry sign, I craned my neck trying to see more, but the overgrown pine trees past the truck made it difficult. I smiled from ear to ear knowing this *thing* we were doing was going to pay off.

"Careful," Tammy said. "Maybe over there." She directed me to an open slot on the side of the road.

I tried to gauge Tammy's excitement level, as mine built to an apex with a 15-year accumulation of procrastination in not doing this sooner. Her expression remained more subdued, possibly concerned for the family that crossed in front of our Jeep.

I slipped into the spot she had pointed out and threw the car in park. I took a heaving deep breath, raised my eyebrows, and smiled. I pulsed with childlike excitement for what lay beyond those trees. I sensed a pleasing validation. I had thrown off the constraints of my alcohol abuse 22 months ago, so that Tammy and I could actually get out and live, so that we could be impulsive and spontaneous, not lethargic and bound.

We got out of the Jeep and looked back towards the entry and above the angled dirt embankment.

"Seriously?" Tammy saw the 160-foot stone tower and dragon-like ornamental structure filling the sky beyond the trees. "*Oh my god.*"

I didn't have the words. I just brimmed with a bemused chuckle. *Ridiculous… This is happening!*

We walked back towards the entry. A rusty crane reached from the beat-up truck, which sat atop flattened tires. A few people gathered around the pickup, taking pictures, documenting and preserving an anticipation that was perhaps equal to mine.

Just beyond the truck-turned-sign, we proceeded towards the grounds, through a massive entry structure displaying a 30-foot archway guardhouse. Immediately, it validated our limited expectations ten times over. We knew instantly that Bishop Castle was going to be way more imposing than we could have conceived when we rebirthed this idea that morning. Made of jagged boulders and stone, the guardhouse-style entry was shaped as if a drawbridge might be able to fill the gigantic opening. Instead, atop the semicircle was an ornate, iron gate that looked like it could drop down to block the magnificent doorway.

But before entering Jim Bishop's property, there was a sign that stood in stark contrast to the natural stone colors that blended nicely with the rocky mountains. The sign was crude, black and white, with a large red STOP admonition, that in its reading mitigated his liability of entering this private property. It read:

STOP

PRIVATE PROPERTY – ENTER AT YOUR OWN RISK!

<u>YOU MUST READ THIS SIGN BEFORE ENTERING</u>

*WE ARE NOT RESPONSIBLE FOR YOUR SAFETY!

*WE ARE NOT RESPONSIBLE FOR YOUR PHYSICAL, MENTAL,

OR EMOTIONAL WELL BEING!

*<u>BISHOP CASTLE IS UNDER CONSTRUCTION!</u>

*PROCEED PAST THIS POINT WITH EXTREME CAUTION!

*YOU MUST KEEP CHILDREN AND PETS UNDER CONTROL AT

ALL TIMES!

*WE RESERVE OUR RIGHT TO FREEDOM OF SPEECH

AND EXPRESSION!

*YOU MIGHT EXPERIENCE FOUL LANGUAGE!

*YOU MIGHT EXPERIENCE STRONGLY EXPRESSIVE BEHAVIOR!

*WE RESERVE OUR RIGHT TO REFUSE ENTRY TO

ANYONE AT ANY TIME!

*IF THE MANAGEMENT OF THIS PROPERTY FEELS

THAT YOU DO NOT AGREE WITH OR HAVE NOT READ THIS SIGN

YOU WILL BE ASKED TO LEAVE!

*IF YOU ARE ASKED BY THE MANAGEMENT OF THIS PROPERTY

TO LEAVE YOU MUST DO SO IMMEDIATELY!

IF YOU DO NOT AGREE WITH ANY OF THESE

CONDITIONS DO NOT ENTER!

IF YOU DO NOT AGREE YOU ARE TRESPASSING!

ENTER AT YOUR OWN RISK!

I had to admit, the sign was refreshing. In an electronic world of 28-page Terms and Service Agreements where you click "I Agree" only to unknowingly sell your child to a corporation, Jim Bishop was clearly letting you know where you stood. This was his property, and by stepping on it, you are agreeing to die on it, or at the very least come out mentally disturbed. Perhaps my cavalier use of Indiana Jones references this morning were not so hokey after all!

Tammy raised her eyebrows with a touch of motherly caution, but my permanent grin was unmoved.

A more weathered, handwritten sign was perched just beyond the first. The impulse to ignore it and move on to the castle was strong, not unlike arriving at Disneyland and wanting to race to The Matterhorn. Given the frightening nature of the first sign, and even our first impressions of the epic scale of this place, it seemed that the small details deserved our respect. We slowed to read it:

Did you know?

Every government official or law enforcement

officer swore an oath to uphold the

Constitution of the United States.

To protect both Life & Liberty. Constitutional

Law is Supreme… not State. Therefore: If

State law conflicts with the Constitution,

which law should the official uphold?

FREEDOM is not FREE. We must fight to be
FREE!

The Founding Fathers expressed to the PEOPLE!!!

"Defending our freedoms in the face of people that
for expedient sake, or behind the guise, for the
welfare and safety of the mases [sic], ignore people's
rights, would forever demand sacrifice & vigilance
from those that desire to be free."

The masses today are begging to not be free.

KNOW YOUR RIGHTS!!!

GOVERN YOUR GOVERNMENT!!!

Tammy and I stood with a reflective pause. The makeshift sign with chipping paint and cracked wood forced a little more concentration in making out the words, but equally, once we teased the message out, it piqued an awkward sense that we needed to pay this Constitutional reference some reverence; at the very least, to try and figure out why it was so important to Jim Bishop and so relevant to his life's work.

"Any thoughts?" Tammy looked in my direction.

"Well," I mused, "I guess recalling what I've heard of this place, local and state authorities are constantly trying to enforce building codes and permits getting Jim Bishop to comply with all sorts of regulations. I think at one point he tried charging visitors to tour the castle, and then the highway officials said he couldn't because of inadequate parking, so now he just takes donations. So, I think he's saying his constitutional rights allow him to do what he wants with his own property, and officials can't trump his rights behind the guise of protecting the 'welfare and safety of the masses.'"

Tammy's eyes widened. "So, we really could be unsafe?"

"Well," I said with a kinky smile, "I guess it depends on what kind of builder he is? We're going to find out."

Jim Bishop's story, his castle, immediately presented a heavy element of "Fuck you!" to the authorities. I related to that persona, a disposition that had entrenched me as I stubbornly continued my drinking...

□ ͏Ϝ Ɓ Ɇ ͏ □

My teenage years were spent listening to musical renegades like Public Enemy, Rage Against the Machine, and Nirvana. I admired the poet Kurt Cobain, who had agreed to appear on the cover of *Rolling Stone* only if he could wear a T-shirt that read, "Corporate Magazines Still Suck."

I gravitated towards writers like Hunter S. Thompson, Matt Taibbi, and Anne Lamott, who had expressive ways of thumbing their noses at the authorities they were addressing.

Even my affection for the Old and New Testament scriptures had me mining the stories of God admonishing farmers not to harvest the entire field, so as to leave crops for the widows and orphans, or Jesus turning over the money changers' tables at the temple, blasting their hypocrisy.

I treated being antiestablishment as a virtue.

It was an advantageous mindset for an addict. Thumbing my nose at the court authorities, taking a drink, and justifying it as a personal freedom. What it really was, was justification in general. If you can frame in your mind a noble purpose in continuing self-harm, it decreases the shame.

With all the same affection and fervor that our relationship had begun with, Tammy and I happily continued to embrace our new life together. We had a brilliantly beautiful and small Fourth of July wedding at our mountain cabin.

Shortly after our honeymoon, I received my driver's license back, my car retrofitted with a breathalyzer.

My community service and group therapy classes were complete. My probation no longer required random urine tests because of my continuously clean results. I was regaining my freedom little by little, to the point where I felt normal again, less restricted. Whenever my leash was extended to a longer length, I would take that adjusted length in the direction of alcohol. Tammy didn't seem to mind and participated with normalcy. I fabricated low-grade justifications for increased use. Since I had to work on a Friday, it was okay to substitute Thursday for Friday... and then drink on Friday and Saturday anyway.

Part of drinking regularly was a collective mindset. We were newlyweds and had been troubled for so long by former partners and work constraints, that we were just enjoying our extended honeymoon. Getting home from work, the clinking of ice in a cocktail glass always preceded the menial tasks of setting car keys on the desk or even removing our shoes. Sometimes with a new IPA, maybe a vodka tonic with lime, or an overfilled glass of wine, nights were supplemented with drinks atop our nightstands, laptop on our bed, binge-watching TV shows that we had missed during the years when we were grinding out a living. We carried this tremendous entitlement that we had missed so much leisure by being responsible over the years; enjoying each other and relaxing was our reward.

Our leisure and laughter were enhanced by alcohol, but so were our arguments. Having been married after a brief one-year courtship left a certain degree of space for us to create elevated misunderstandings. I would treat simple questions from her as indictments or insecurities, and drinking would only provide the fuel to inflame what could have been an immediate reconciliation.

I had miscalculated, with Tammy having adult children in their twenties, that Nathan would be the only child in need of raising. Increasingly, her children levied burdens on our time and finances that I hadn't expected, disappointments that were carelessly vocalized when the liquor would loosen my judgment.

I had a firm false sense of security from knowing that my drinking wasn't even close to problematic, given that I had seen what that looked like in years prior. I also knew that, because I'd had few issues in complying with the court-ordered restrictions, I could quit whenever I wanted. My alcohol problems in the past were not a problem with alcohol, per se; it was a problem of my past circumstances, my environment. Now that my relationship environment was resolved, save for the aberrational argument, I transitioned from the pains of apathy and betrayal, to the comfort of vibrancy and love; I was free to use alcohol with normalcy.

It did seem, though, that daily I still felt an undercurrent of preoccupation as to whether we would or would not be having drinks each night. When we did choose to drink, I experienced micro-moments where I was reminded that I did not have the control that I thought I did.

After a particular night of drinking, I begrudgingly awoke to get Nathan to school. Surprisingly, my car's breathalyzer, registered an egregious red light and a harsh "FAIL" notification. *Fail? I still have alcohol in my system?* Embarrassed and caught off guard, my answer was not to abstain on school nights, but to buy a separate handheld breathalyzer, so that I could pre-test myself and never show the authorities a registered "FAIL" notice again. A sick primal satisfaction pulsed through me whenever I circumvented the system.

This tango went on for a few years past our wedding where we were living, loving, laughing, and drinking. As with any tango, our third wheel of a dance partner, alcohol, presented moments of bliss and grace, along with opportunities to trip up and look like a fool.

As time passed, Nathan crept closer to driving age. His mom had moved closer and gotten engaged again, and he now split his time more evenly between us. Co-parenting was civil, income levels were stable, and my relationship with Tammy flourished beyond my wildest expectations. Before now, I had never dreamt of this type of contentment and solidarity with another person.

Three years into our marriage, Tammy and I began entertaining the idea of moving up to our cabin full time. Many reasons compelled us to make the change. It was something we could do together and make it our own. Our suburban home was at that 15-year mark where all of the projects were dated, expensive, and unsexy, like the roof shingles and paint in need of replacement. Our community didn't have the same feel either that it did when I'd been married to Mindy. Some friends had not survived the housing market collapse, but the ones that stayed now treated me like my known indiscretions with alcohol had branded me with a scarlet letter. They were uncomfortable drinking around me, and I was all too aware and conscious of it myself. Moving up to the cabin would provide the same type of reset that I had enjoyed by marrying Tammy; I will just reset my community and enjoy alcohol with the same increased normalcy I was experiencing with her.

I wasn't intentionally hellbent on manipulating my situation towards alcohol. I certainly had the cognitive dissonance that allowed me to believe that changing my environment would help me decrease my use. I optimistically thought that having a smaller home and fewer bills would decrease stress, and thereby also decrease use, and I assumed that removing myself from all the past reminders of my turmoil would help, as well. It was such a mental obsession, constantly trying to dial in the appropriate use and non-use, dancing between the right and the wrong of it all.

We proceeded with our ambitious plan of downsizing a 15-year-old home. We allocated some of our more expensive furniture and electronics to Tammy's kids, young adults who could certainly use them. We had a Craigslist fire sale where people poached whatever we wouldn't be able to fit in our modest cabin. I sifted through 20 years of memories that had accumulated in our crawlspace, applying heartfelt gratitude for Mindy, my friends, my family, and my former life, peppered with stings of resentment and abandonment.

Within the first week of moving to the cabin, settled in and content, I remember one weekday night when Tammy and I sat in front of the fireplace, watching TV and drinking. In spite of the evening's pleasantness, I was subdued, and I think that Tammy sensed this. "Anything wrong?" she asked.

Upholding my principle to always be honest and vulnerable with her, I said, "I guess I'm a little disappointed in myself." I dragged my index finger along the rim of my cocktail glass, then lifted it and tilted it towards Tammy. "I wasn't expecting this to follow me up here."

I must have been delusional to think that my relationship with alcohol was somehow external, to suppose that a geographical cure would unlock the secret door to a moderation that continued to elude me. Now, with decreased bills, a flourishing and increasing love for my wife, and happiness beyond measure, my desire to combat alcohol continued to be a puzzle I could not solve.

I yielded to a flimsy will and drank daily from that moment forward.

□ ˝F ฿ €˝ □

Tammy and I crossed the threshold of the caution signs and stepped underneath the massive circular entry. In awe, we looked up, curious as to what was holding the stones in place. Rocks lined up perfectly with hand-mixed mortar and the occasional protruding rebar. To the right of the structure was a staircase, lined with handpicked boulders leading to the top of the guard station. Within the guard station were a woodburning stove and a rigged electric garage door opener, which must have controlled the elaborate iron gate.

I felt like a boy, getting to climb into my friend's treehouse for the first time, knowing I was allowed to play inside the imagination of another's mind. I fizzled with the excitement to see more.

We departed the upper platform from a different set of stairs that led to an open courtyard, where Bishop Castle was on full display. The aesthetic splendor was indescribable; that one man was purported to be responsible for its grandeur, emboldened my inner skeptic.

We circled to the left of the courtyard, identifying a small staircase that would lead us up the hill upon which the castle was perched. The perimeter land was littered with industrious generators, RVs, shacks, and cement mixers. We bypassed a tired, elderly gentleman whose frail stature did not afford him the mobility to join the others on a tour of the castle. He sat in a folding chair beside his dog, who didn't appear to be in much better shape.

As we stopped to get a full-scale panoramic view of the castle, I overheard a young father tell his small son, "It's okay. Just go stand by him. I want to get you and him in a picture."

My jaw dropped. I had dismissed the older gentleman as a weathered traveler, a vagrant that blended in with the dated rusty tools resting along the margins of the property. *Could it be… Was this Jim Bishop? He did all this?*

I looked at him closer, and then swiveled back to the castle. It seemed unimaginable, so I watched, gleaning additional clues as the young father prompted his little boy to stand by the man.

I took a step towards the father and whispered, "Is that him? He did this?"

"Yeah. That's Jim Bishop," the father confirmed. "I guess he makes it up here now on the weekends and watches people tour everything."

I reached for the father's phone. "Here, would you like to be in the picture?" Then I held up the phone, looked to the hardened man, and asked, "Sir, is it okay?"

Jim Bishop looked indifferent as he gave a slight nod. I took a couple of pictures with the father on one side and his son on the other. Jim Bishop removed himself from the chair to stand for the photos, and in doing so, a slouched frame transformed into a stocky, solid stature. In no way did he want to present as meager. He was perhaps five-foot-five, but had a small curve of the upper back where time and wear had stolen a couple of inches. He boasted a one hundred percent blue-collar appearance; a thick, overgrown mustache dominated a sun-leathered face of stubble, with a flannel shirt, soiled blue jeans, and work boots completing his frame. Throughout this exchange, in contrast to the smiling father and son, Mr. Bishop's face remained stoic.

I handed the phone back to the father, but my eyes were on Jim Bishop. I tried to discern whether there was any joy in him, but his scowl led to the uncomfortable feeling that we were intruding. I kindly nodded and said, "Thank you, sir."

Jim Bishop and I squared ourselves up towards a full viewing of Bishop Castle. We were together. We stood, silent, taking it in.

The uncertainty I once had about a solitary man building an enormous castle in the Colorado mountains evaporated. At that moment, I mentally conjoined Jim Bishop's drive and determination with my own sobriety; standing here today, we were both proof that anything is possible.

I shook my head in awe, looking up at the otherworldly metaphor of passion and self-determination blistering in the forest.

"I mean it, sir," I said. *"Thank you."*

Jeff Bowersox

Chapter 8

The Castle

2:30 PM

Tammy and I linked hands as we approached Bishop Castle, studying the human activity above to determine what other people's interests were. The view from our position in the courtyard presented a narrow cement staircase that ascended the first third of the castle about 50 feet above.

The base of the castle that anchored the four main corners of the structure looked tremendously solid. From the top of the staircase, the bottom portion tapered down on all sides and flared out, presenting in the same fashion as The Eiffel Tower. The base was bold, boasting crudely honed Rocky Mountain boulders, reddish-brown, weighing probably 50 pounds apiece. Each footing curved upwards in an archway-type fashion.

Following the footings from left to right, and then looking up, we stared at the front of the castle, which delivered a dramatic view of a metallic dragon neck and head that protruded, leaning into the sky. Panning from the right, back to the left, the upper-back of Bishop Castle displayed its tallest cylinder tower, the equivalent height of a 13-story building. The back towers were decoratively capped with artistic metal scaffolding and linked together with iron bridgework.

We remained silent, taking it all in from the ground.

I was keenly aware that I brushed shoulders with human ingenuity daily—our roads and highways, my bank building, the electronics in my vehicle, my cellphone — but I understood that it takes hundreds, if not thousands, of people to bring those miracles from concept to creation.

If Tammy and I muttered anything, they were blurbs like, "*No way... Unreal... Geez...*"

The unmentioned astonishment was that the elderly fellow that I had just interacted with was responsible for all of this. No architects, no engineering team, no fleet of trucks delivering materials, no heavy machine operators, and no day laborers. Just Jim Bishop. Or, as the website said, Jim Bishop *and the hand of God*.

We approached the straight staircase with caution, already determining that if anyone were descending then it would be a tight fit for them to pass by. The narrowness and pitch of the staircase begged the obvious:

modern building codes and safeguards would not come into play.

Stopping at the base, we inspected the black wrought iron handrail for its structural integrity. We paused at the first step, forced not only to look up the stairs, but beyond, revealing a distant view of others traversing the metal bridgework that attached to the towers.

Taking the first step defied reason. If you saw a handful of people climbing at the top of a rollercoaster, you would immediately run and find some qualified personnel to go get them down. But we were here, and the other visitors were doing it... *It's why we were here.*

Single file, we began to climb the staircase.

Jim Bishop bought this parcel of land for $450 when he was 15 years old. He had saved money from odd jobs, cutting lawns and delivering papers. Too young to buy it himself, he convinced his parents to sign on. He spent the rest of his teen years and early twenties clearing an area of trees, enjoying the mountainous property nestled 9,000 feet above sea level.

Jim Bishop married Phoebe at the age of 23 in 1967, and two years later, he would begin the modest task of building a one-room family cottage on his property. Noticing the abundance of natural rocks and stones, he used the easily at-hand materials to lay the first course of his foundation.

Over time, passing travelers would stop and ask Jim what he was doing, noting that due to his use of stone, it looked like he was building a castle. And so the idea of Bishop Castle was conceived.

Jim Bishop had all the underpinnings to take on such a project; he loved spending his summers on his property, and it wasn't essential that any sort of structure be entirely habitable, given that he had a proper home and career 40 miles to the northeast. Lending to the ability to add to his fledgling castle, Jim's family business in town was in the ornamental iron business, a resource and trade that would tie in beautifully with his growing architectural ambitions.

Blueprints or formal building permits were never a consideration. It was Jim Bishop's land, and he would do with it what he pleased.

Tammy and I reached the first level after climbing the staircase. We stood for a moment, catching our breath and looking back down the steps to survey the surrounding land. The platform-like concourse at the top of the stairs was made of interwoven metal that flexed slightly when we stepped on it. Recalling the warning signs upon entry, I proceeded with caution.

Our heads were continually on a swivel. Everything here stood in sharp contrast to the sea of familiar, cookie-cutter homes that we had driven through two hours before. My eyes darted from the mortar that held each boulder in place to the iron window inlays that gave us our first peek inside. I ran my fingers down the bar of the window, giving it a slight tug, adding to my data bank of micro-confirmations that the scope and aesthetic of this place was real.

I studied the exclusivity of the architecture, but also found myself intrigued by the dozens of people on the property. Strangers and I exchanged smiles as we passed, in silent solidarity that we were uncovering this mystery together.

We eagerly made our first entry into the main room of the castle. Breathtaking. The grand ballroom held the bulk of the castle's insides. Maybe 75-by-75-foot square, it gloriously confused us as to where we should look first.

Above us were hand-milled wood beams from the native pine trees. They were supporting iron bracing and an A-frame cathedral ceiling, constructed entirely of see-through material. The pristine blue Colorado sky and wispy clouds bounced light into every area of the castle. We walked to the center of the room, where Tammy circled in place, taking in an internal panorama of the beauty. The genuineness of her grin put to bed any insecurities I'd had about this journey being too one-sided in favor of my liking.

The front wall of the ballroom boasted ornate glass doors with stained glass panels. Intricate steel levers wrapped the glass, enabling the opening of the doors to the outside veranda. Following the majestic doors above, it was clear that there was a chimney connected to the dragon neck and head that we'd seen earlier. It calmed my inner panic, that for all of the intensity of the warning signs and the stern interaction with Mr. Bishop, there was a fantastical inner child that had him playfully making his life's work a living, breathing monument.

I broke the silence. "A castle with a fire breathing dragon in the middle of nowhere. Sounds about right." I widened my eyes sarcastically.

The room drew us to a thin corridor revealing a spiral staircase heading upward.

"You ready?" I asked, now fully aware that Tammy was still nervous.

We worked our way up the tight staircase. Fellow castle goers worked their way down and we committed to a tight squeeze, mentally trying to determine which of us had the right of way. In all, we realized that with no set rules, we made our own, joyfully navigating the reality that this place was not built to code.

The concrete spiraled steps, encased in the boulder-walled cylinder, eluded the sun. While I struggled for appropriate footing, my eyes searched for spots where I thought that Tammy might hit her head. The scope of the building parameters were suited to Jim Bishop's five-and-a-half-foot frame, but didn't have Tammy's six-foot-two size in mind.

She tends to be resilient, deflecting with what she calls "tall jokes," which are actually cleverly disguised short jokes with a good PR spin. "This place must be really big for guys like you and Mr. Bishop. You two could confuse a hobbit house for a castle."

"Tall joke?" I asked, knowing the answer.

"Tall joke," she confirmed.

We emerged at the top of the second-tallest tower. Whereas moments before we had been on the ground staring at the small people in the sky, we now stood in their place. Any exterior platforms were made of the same iron mesh material, creating a veranda that wrapped around the external circle of the stone tower.

Steadily accruing a collection of pictures on our phones, I knew better than to ask Tammy to join me on the arching bridge that connected the two towers. I loved the idea of our picture together way up in the sky, but my fear that she would turn back kept me mute. The bridge was admittedly a little sketchy. I gently worked my way out to the center, and as I stood waiting to have my picture taken, I felt it wobble as others moved around the interconnected iron scaffolding below.

Next, we navigated to the back corner of Bishop Castle and reached the uppermost point of the tallest tower. At no point in our meanderings were we disappointed.

We joined two other tourists already at the top, a middle-aged couple from Texas. As with any of the handful of people we interacted with, our conversation was warm and friendly.

The wife explained how they had been here about 20 years ago but drove out of their way today to see the progress.

"Was he working on it back then?" I asked.

"Oh my, yes." Her eyes brightened. "You should have seen him. He'd free climb and scale the wall, no harness. He'd put a stone in place. He'd hang from the iron work and swing to his next area of work. It was amazing to watch. None of this portion was done," she said, gesturing. "Is this your first time here?"

"Yeah." I paused, embarrassed. "I mean, I feel like I've known about it for a long time, but I just never really got around to coming out here to see if it was real."

After the couple had departed, Tammy and I stood overlooking the serenity of the castle from its highest perch. As we watched the deep green pine trees bend in the slight breeze, an eruption of verbal chaos echoed from the dirt courtyard below.

"You have no idea where it's fucking going! You have no idea what they are taking from you!"

The bolt of screaming incited a prickly sense of danger. We leaned over the iron rail, looking into the courtyard and trying to identify the source of commotion below us. Tammy surveyed the visitors, watching them stop in their tracks or scurry to get a closer view.

Jim Bishop paced away from his chair, his voice at full volume. From our vantage point 13 stories up, he appeared to be wagging his finger. We could only make out a few of the bold utterances, but we could hear the shouts.

"Oh yeah, you let them take your money to build their empire, but you won't hold them accountable when they take the money to cure your cancer! You're dead! You're dead and they're fat!"

Tammy looked at me, concerned. "Do you think he's okay?"

"Well," I said with a slight undercurrent of satisfaction that the entry's warning signs of strong opinions were unfolding below, "I mean…?" I shrugged.

Mr. Bishop walked towards the front of the castle beyond our view. "What do you expect! What do all you people expect when it comes…? …there it… fucking… anyway! You can't…"

The topic was too distant to decipher, bolts of cusswords not lending any clarity. We stood in silent observation, never imagining that being 160 feet in the air would feel like the safest place to be.

I studied Mr. Bishop as he returned towards the back of his castle. He stepped quietly now, but with vigor, tossing a water bottle into a metal trash drum with force. I examined the majestic castle that he had created. I'm not sure what he believed in, but I could take some wide swings and probably correctly hit on a few of his ideas.

I reflected as I stood there. There was a time when I believed emphatically in social ideas, in the sciences, in dogmatic church communities, in God, but towards the end of my relationship with alcohol, I'm not sure if I believed in anything at all…

◻ ˝F ฿ €˝ ◻

Entering our fourth summer as a married couple, Tammy and I had comfortably settled into our new life. The three of us, including Nathan, had made the adjustment to our mountain cabin, an 875-square-foot home on five acres about 25 minutes from Nathan's high school. We were close enough to our former community that we could engage in the same modern fashion to which Nathan was accustomed, but far away enough that our life didn't carry the full weight and expense of the Denver market.

Nathan obtained his driver's license and added his own Jeep to our fleet, which gave him flexibility to come to the mountains or stay closer to town with his Mom. His grades were solid, and his peer groups were both studious and virtuous.

We were living mortgage-free, with minimal financial constraints. Tammy worked from home and I ran into town nightly to tend to my business and support my staff.

The local connections in our mountain community flourished. The Sprucewood, a bar just down the dirt road from our home, acted more like a community center, a family gathering place.

There was a renegade sensibility to our community. Our mountain people loathed conformity, hated houses built on top of each other and the beauty of Colorado being paved over to build a new Hobby Lobby. I rather enjoyed the solidarity in their views, given the distasteful exit from my suburban experiment. The promises of perfect living were a con game, and the veil had been lifted to expose the fraud.

We didn't need a supermarket down the street. Often a surplus of freshly laid eggs would appear on your doorstep, delivered by a neighbor from down the road.

I wouldn't say that we were living "off-grid," but it contrasted starkly to climbing the suburban social hierarchy that I had known in the years before.

I had left everything behind, all of the disappointments. In my twenties, I was so full of ideas and had encountered so many people with respectable, principled passions.

I don't know, maybe time had made me a cynic. I had encountered a revered scientist who was committed to changing the world, but who verbally assaulted his wife in public. I had seen a pastor teach about unconditional love, only to stand up in church and blame a divorced couple that were living together for our lack of church growth. I had experienced my deeply religious wife, whose main contribution to our union had been her faithfulness, screw a real estate agent during a weekend fling.

I, at one point, entered a court-ordered AA meeting and handed the leader my attendance record to sign, only to have it thrown back at me. "We only want people who want to be here." *Who said I didn't want to be there?*

I'd had friends who had been like brothers and sisters, who I had opened my home to every week, who no longer invited me over.

Over time, I had managed to find the people with dogmatic, passionate ideas to be the most disappointing. They invited despair. I expected more out of the folks who were the most vocal about their ethics.

It made sense, then, to hit reset and be with the person I loved, in a sparse community where I could keep disappointments at a comfortable distance. But here's the thing: the despair and grief travel like a virus, and I was their host.

For all the measures I had taken to rebuild my world and minimize environmental stressors, it didn't take long to realize that my grief had come along for the ride, and that pouring liquor over it nightly was the only answer I knew to make it go away. My solution, with repetitive and addictive consistency, was to start with a double vodka tonic, escaping into the blissful, unconditional acceptance of my wife and forgetting about the past.

I didn't feel like the intensity of my drinking could reach the horrific extent that it had in years prior. The car accident and the DUI were almost purposeful acts of self-destruction, signaling to my remaining loved ones my pain and brokenness.

I was okay now, exactly where I was. I had removed myself from reminders of judgment and designed my world so that I could continue drinking without feeling the shame from others. But I found that the same aggravation I felt towards the dogmatic people who had let me down, was an aggravation that I uncomfortably had to apply to myself. We judge most harshly in others what is most true in us.

I was the one who spent his twenties and thirties believing that productivity and people-pleasing held the key to some reciprocal utopia. *I believed and preached moderation and self-control.* Perhaps the grief and disappointment I attributed to other's actions were really disgust and shame at my own choices, at my own inability to control this social conductor called alcohol. *What was wrong with me?*

That summer had all the external benchmarks of paradise in our marriage: love, in a relationship that was physically and intellectually vibrant; security, in a gorgeous, debt-free home nestled in the Colorado mountains; and hope, in a thriving and well-adjusted child entering into adulthood with his own visions and dreams. And although I strived to continually recreate this "sweet spot," I still found myself increasing my alcohol consumption.

In the evenings was when I would manage my business affairs. If I had everything well under control, no matter the day of the week, I could pat myself on the back and find it worthy of a celebration. I would cook dinner and start with a cocktail. Tammy would be wrapping up her work from home, and as the clock neared 5:00, I would slide a drink in her direction. Drinks were free flowing for us both after that, but I was acutely aware that I was refilling my glass more often than she was, and with more alcohol each time.

Closer to bedtime, as Tammy would be in the bathroom getting ready for bed, I would pull one more shot as a night cap to assure my sound sleep.

Daily, although I trimmed my work and household responsibilities to a minimum, the simplest of tasks, like balancing the business books, began to give me anxiety. I found annoyance in the most menial tasks. I was groggy and wet-brained, and it seemed like my attitude and countenance was in a holding pattern, waiting to get back to the evening where I could adjust it with more drinks.

The outdoors of our home boasted an unbridled number of creative activities. We had mountain hikes, world-class fly fishing, and ATVs, yet nothing creative or exciting happened. Maybe I'd lay out on the deck, get a little sun, and convince myself and others that I was in a leisure paradise; what I was actually doing was killing time until the evening, when I could alter my mood and feed my growing addiction.

This pattern grew. Drink. Sloth. Anxiety. Guilt. Shame. Repeat... Over time, every element of this cycle increased in intensity.

The scariest part is when you stop making justifications for your use. You spent enough time drinking to celebrate, drinking to grieve, drinking to hide... Drinking because of the highs, because of the boredom, because of the lows... It's frightening when you become tired of the mental gymnastics of convincing yourself that you drink because of a reason, and instead you resolve that you are the reason. You drink because this is *who you are.*

In a way, it's also a relief. You are no longer forced to stand at a podium, purporting to live moderately and in control. You no longer have two rivals struggling for the will of your brain.

This is *who you are.* You're an addict, and mentally coming to terms with that provided less turmoil than pretending you weren't.

□″F ₿ €″□

Tammy and I stood at the top of Jim Bishop's personal creation of paradise. His castle, a monument of freedom. I dragged my finger along the railing and followed its licorice-like curve, thinking of the moment when he must have forged this piece of iron. I reflected on my days of recreating my own personal paradise, its external promises of happiness always yielding to the torment of my hypocrisy.

Beyond my finger, looking down, Jim Bishop casually returned from the trash drum to his chair. His strong opinions on personal freedoms and not letting oppressive entities hold him back were made manifest in creating his castle. But maybe more unique than the castle itself, was the man who made it, a person who found his truth, stood for it, and spent his days putting it into action.

Hypocrisy is everywhere. I identified it in others all the time. I loathed it in myself when I drank.

This day though, sober, I looked down at Mr. Bishop and identified with his integrity.

I knew my truth now. I knew I was acting it out.

Chapter 9

The Basement

<u>3:35 PM</u>

Tammy and I stood perched at Bishop Castle's highest point. "Well," I said, "should we work our way to the bottom?"

Although it was still light out, the sun prematurely gave way to the expansive native trees. We headed down the back tower, pausing one last time inside the Grand Ballroom.

Tammy noticed that the spiral staircase went further down than just the main level and leaned over to investigate. "Should we go down this way so we don't miss anything?"

"Sure!" I swiveled in mid-stride towards Tammy, stoked to extend our adventure.

The staircase eerily dropped into a dark and unfinished underside of the castle. Save for a generator and a few tools tucked into corners, the space was bare, largely unused.

From the underside of the castle, I peered out east. "It looks like he thought of making a moat out in front. See how the dirt is all engineered like a trench? This portion here must just be a basement or something?"

Tammy put her hand suggestively near my inseam. "*Noooo.*" She leaned into my ear. "I think it's *the dungeon…*"

Chapter 10

The Gift Shop

4:10 PM

We made our way out of... err, the dungeon, which positioned us at the gravel base in front of the castle. Looking up like a child, I knew the metallic dragon head should be hovering way above me as I tilted towards the sky. I took a pensive moment. My eyes became misty.

Twenty-one months ago, I had begun the battle for sobriety, wanting to quit drinking simply so that I wouldn't die. I had no idea at the time that an indirect consequence would be the reality of *actually living*. The awareness struck me; today, I was living.

We proceeded south, returning to the courtyard. As if the outburst had never taken place, Jim Bishop idly sat in his lawn chair, with the same stoic gaze towards his castle, the same mangy companion at his feet.

As we walked towards him, Tammy said softly, "I feel like I want to tell him how happy he's made us. His creation has brought so much joy today."

"I don't know," I said. "I just feel like he might be a little volatile right now."

We walked past Mr. Bishop, trying to make eye contact, offering our sincerest smiles. I think we both hoped that we might see even a slight opening from him, maybe a quick gaze that welcomed further interaction. But he sat, unmoved, eyes fixed on his otherworldly castle.

We breezed past him towards our final stop before leaving: the gift shop.

Despite being made of combined modular storage sheds, the gift shop felt warm and expansive. Bishop Castle has been solely funded by donations from the visitors and the money made at the gift shop. Where I would normally be afraid of getting financially taken for a ride in such a place, the value in my experience today prodded me to empty my pockets without hesitation.

The lady behind the counter kindly greeted us upon entry. The gift shop boasted an assortment of hats, scarves, toys, knives, jewelry, and postcards of the castle. We casually strolled towards the back, where Tammy locked eyes on the necklaces and pendants.

She turned over a couple of price tags, sensitive to my frugality. Suppressing my usual inclination towards thriftiness, I said, "Make sure you get whatever you want.

It'll be nice to have keepsakes from our day. I'm going to go look at the pocketknives."

Tammy picked out a couple of items and made her way towards the glass counter where I hovered over the variety of knives.

Tammy beamed at the attendant behind the counter. "What a day! Our trip out here has been such an unexpected shock. Have you worked here long?"

"Going on thirty years," she said brightly. "Yeah, I've seen quite the transformation of this place over the years."

Tammy kept gushing, "Never in our wildest expectations did we think the castle would be so beautiful. The expanse of it is amazing."

"It really is something else," she affirmed, as if she'd heard this many times before. "The castle has come with its share of sacrifices though, that's for sure."

"Does Mr. Bishop still work on it?" Tammy asked.

"He still piddles around a little. I wasn't sure if he'd come up this weekend. He lost Phoebe to cancer a couple of weeks ago. Married over 50 years. I think he just feels closer to them when he's here."

"Them?" Tammy asked.

"He lost his little boy here. An accident they had pulling one of the trees out of the ground. Like I said, what you see out there came with its fair share of sacrifice and hardship… as is life, I guess. There were days that I thought Jim was going to build that tower until it reached the heavens, just so he could see his son again."

There were a few beats of silence, and then Tammy said, "I hope he knows, even given the sacrifices, he must have touched thousands of people? The scale of this place… what a single person can accomplish?"

"Oh, honey, I think he knows. We've had people who come here year after year. People who struggle. Artists needing a breakthrough of inspiration. People mourning, wanting to tie in a happy memory with a lost loved one. Folks get married, making this place the symbol of really building something grand. People who've overcome addictions, needing to remind themselves that all things are possible. I know I've just ran the gift shop in my lifetime, but every day I come away with a new story about how people who are stagnant or complacent, learning that they can achieve something exceptional."

Tammy let the words sink in, then directed her eyes to my search.

"Can I take a look at this one right there?" I pointed.

I checked its heft as if I knew something about knives. I loved it. It had a blue titanium frame that housed gray gun-brushed metal insides. "I'll take this one. It's unique. It'll remind me of his castle," I said, smiling at our host.

After depositing a sizable donation, our mementos in tow, we exited, asking the gift shop attendant to please extend our thanks to Mr. Bishop. In no real hurry, and not wanting our journey to be over, we stood outside the shop taking in one more full panoramic view of the unimaginable: Bishop Castle.

A few minutes later, we worked our Jeep away from its makeshift parking spot and cornered it back and forth to get it heading back in the direction of home. Tammy and I may have exhausted our words, or maybe in the moment we found words to be insufficient. A deep, profound satisfaction rested in our silence.

As we headed back north on the winding road towards home, the sun gave way to the Colorado mountain range. Wispy clouds that had formerly shown white through the castle's glass ceiling, now blasted in shimmering orange.

Staring through the windshield, I held a purposeful moment of silence for the loss of Jim Bishop's wife and son. As we walked past him that last time, I'd felt the sting of any earlier prejudgments that I'd had about his somber gaze. The idea that I had any accurate interpretation of Jim Bishop's emotions was foolish. I had no idea he had just lost his wife and that the grounds we had just gleefully toured had taken his child.

As if the vehicle's soundtrack knew our mood, the soft plucking of the ukulele from an indie band started playing over the speakers. It went on for a few bars, and without us exchanging words, Tammy joined me with the same introspection. The gentle intro of the ukulele strings strummed way too heavily.

She pressed stop on the song.

That same song played two years ago, when we were closer to death's door than we had ever been...

◻᾿F ℬ Є᾿◻

Tammy and I spent the day outdoors on our five-acre mountain property. A soft acoustic mix from the Bluetooth speaker melted into the trickle of the creek that ran alongside our home. I pulled away a heavy carpet of pine needles with a rake while she freed unwelcome foliage from her flower bed by hand. We goofed off and laughed as the hose that watered our flowers kept finding the nozzle pointed in one another's direction.

Even considering my former stumbles, legal troubles, and disappointments involving alcohol, that late summer afternoon was "the why" in which I drank. In its proper context, alcohol could enhance a good time, could always offer the promise of making it better.

Firm in my resolution, for better or worse, I was a daily drinker. And for me, this day was the better. There didn't seem to be a more perfect cap to a warm, productive day outdoors than to imbibe multiple drinks at dinner.

Over time, I had learned that I should only drink when there wasn't a chance of driving drunk, a mistake that I never wanted to repeat again. But I seemed to always be designing those moments, when we could isolate at home, drinking, not having to experience the world around us.

Although my drinking looked normal from the outside, I was starting to build a few shameful secrets.

"I'm thinking some Long Island Iced Teas on the deck before dinner?" I delivered it as more of a statement than a question.

I poured us a couple of drinks that evening to get us started, but I quickly guzzled my first one down, refilled it, and brought them out as if it were my first. Any happiness that occurred during the day could not compete with the relief in my brain after downing that first glass.

Within a minute, I would feel the silent alarm of a dull pain under my rib cage. I found myself rubbing the underside of my sore liver daily, only for it to flare up intensely upon first consumption. Another silent secret I was keeping to myself.

My intellectual understanding that I had long been affecting a vital organ, never seemed to hold the weight it should have when the time came to manipulate my brain chemistry. My addicted brain always convinced me that poisoning myself somehow meant survival, liver be damned.

I brought our drinks out to the deck, and Tammy and I giddily pulled ourselves up on the chaise lounges. We clinked our glasses together just as the phone rang.

Tammy slipped inside to answer it.

"What? No! No! What? Oh my God… Where?" I had never heard Tammy's voice like that before, and I could tell that something was wrong.

I jumped up, trying to interpret one side of a frantic conversation. I gleaned enough information that I decided to head to the bedroom to remove my soiled gardening clothes; we were going somewhere.

She was crying and shaking as she hung up the phone. Tammy's daughter, Jeri, who lived out in a north suburb of Denver, had had a life-threatening stroke.

I couldn't speak to the myriad of worries and emotions Tammy had going on in her mind. I couldn't even fully devote my attention to wrapping my head around the story she was trying to tell me. I wasn't able to give her my undivided care, because at the forefront of my thoughts was, *I'm about to knowingly drive under the influence for the first time since my arrest five years ago.*

I weighed the understanding that, with my high alcohol tolerance, having had one drink before we left was not a driving hazard. But it was the principle of it. I had vowed never to put myself in a situation where I would do that again. I would maintain the control over alcohol and be cautious, always playing the game of predicting my circumstances.

I contemplated having Tammy drive us to the hospital, knowing that she hadn't even taken a sip of alcohol yet, but my ego and my growing secrecy did not want to reveal that I had primed my brain before we'd even made it outside. I felt that in her state of hysteria, I was still the safest option to get us to the hospital 65 miles away.

For all of the ways I had designed my circumstances to be free—free to drink, free from other's judgments, free from being overly responsible—I found that I wasn't free at all. I wasn't free to give the love of my life my unhindered attention, I wasn't free to take my hands from the ten-and-two position of the steering wheel, and I wasn't free to speed and get her to the hospital faster. I was a slave.

We arrived at the hospital safely. As the stepdad of an adult child, I hadn't had a lot of opportunities to get to know Jeri. I courteously stayed to the side of the waiting room while Tammy and her immediate family gathered information.

In critical condition, but stable enough to travel the following day, Jeri was airlifted to a Denver hospital with an ICU that specialized in head and neck trauma.

Tammy spent a couple of days with Jeri, sleeping by her side in the ICU. The doctors put her on blood thinners and started to assess that her speech and motor functions were doing well. I would head home in the evening, taking care of any business on the way, and return with fresh clothes and food each day. After a couple of stable days, we were hopeful for recovery.

I returned home each night unable to sleep. I was on standby for Tammy, which compelled me not to drink at night while I was home, in case she needed to summon me to the hospital. The daily emotional rollercoaster combined with my ill-adjusted body chemistry left me irritable, longing for a fix.

By day three, I felt like Jeri's condition was predictable enough that I picked up a bottle of vodka on the way home. Through the whole ordeal, I can't count the number of times that I pondered whether or not I could have a drink. If you had asked me, I would have said I was relieved that Jeri was getting better, and that Tammy might be able to come home soon, but in reality, I was more relieved that I might be able to continue drinking back at my normal levels.

Going home on that third night, with my bottle of coping mechanism saddled in my passenger seat, Tammy called and frantically asked me to return. Jeri had just suffered multiple additional strokes and the prognosis of her making it through alive was bleak.

Shame coursed through my body. My heart sank. For a moment, I was upset that I wasn't going to get to drink.

I turned around and headed back to the hospital. But I'd had the thought... I had selfishly let my addicted brain speak, clouding over the heart I was supposed to have for my loved ones.

I drove back to the hospital, terrified and sick to my stomach at who I had become.

I settled into the ICU waiting room that evening. Tammy emerged from the care unit and tried to explain the unexplainable. Her sobbing made it impossible to understand the medical information she was relaying. She buried her head in my chest, and the wet puddle left on my sweatshirt said everything she couldn't.

After a while, she sat up. "I'm going to go stay by her side tonight."

"Of course. I'll be here."

Around 1AM, I was beginning to doze off in the dark, uninhabited waiting room. I was abruptly startled by the bustle of a large woman, a visitor I had spotted sharing our space earlier, frantically moving her way through the waiting room. She hit the coded keypad to the door to gain access to the patient rooms. She nervously mishit the buttons.

"No, no, no." She started banging on the door. "Please! Nooooo!" She crumpled to her knees with a desperate slap on the door, crying and wailing.

I postured up and assumed she had received horrible news of a family member.

Another lady immediately entered the waiting room, her car keys jingling in her hand as she scurried to her aid. Without a doubt, we all knew what was behind that door: death. And although I had calculated and created my perfect environment, convincing myself that nothing bad could ever happen, life's finality was upon us that night. *Death was real.*

A steady procession of loved ones started filling the waiting room. Priority family members went straight back to the deceased, while others nestled into the empty chairs around me. At one point, a man who was perhaps a brother of the deceased came back out of the patient rooms, kicking a trash can and launching it across the room. Our waiting room had turned into a triage of grief.

I selfishly prayed under my breath that our family wouldn't be next.

Morning broke early. Tammy joined me in the waiting room, slumping as she sat. Her face was swollen, her eyes red and heavy. "Did you get any sleep?" she asked.

"Not much. It was pretty horrific out here last night," I said softly.

"Yeah, it was a terror listening to all those poor folks wailing," she said.

"How's Jeri? What are they saying?"

"It's not good, Jeff. The strokes were massive, but they identified that they were happening immediately. They opened the artery to get blood flow to the brain, but they don't know the extent of the new brain damage. Worse, the doctor thinks the clots are just going to keep happening." Tammy melted into my arms, sobbing. "The doctor said there's a slim chance she'll make it."

Jeri's dad, siblings, and close friends started pouring into the waiting room. They were here earlier than normal, their expedient shuffle comprehending the urgency. "Hey," I said, giving up my seat. "I'll go get us some coffees."

When I returned, I turned the corner towards the hub of the quiet ICU waiting room where everyone had congregated. Carrying eight coffees atop two cardboard trays, a strange sound started to fill the room. It sounded like... *musical organs*? Loud enough that everyone turned my direction, the confusion continued with what sounded like some sort of *talking*?

Picking up on the tones of what it was way before everyone else, I realized it was the start of the Prince song, "Let's Go Crazy." The song starts with what would sound like any delivery to a funeral service... *Dearly beloved, we are gathered here today to get through this thing called life...*

Confused, my head jerked around, trying to determine its source. I panned all around, wondering where and why it was playing. Jeri's family members didn't. *They just kept looking at me.* Confused, I lifted the trays of coffee and stared at my pants... *It was coming from me?* The song was playing from my phone.

Quickly, I tried to find a place to set the coffees down. I was trying so hard to be a non-intrusive member of our gathering. Here I stood, somehow, filling the quiet, tense room with Prince? Sounds of a funeral service?

I grabbed my phone, looked at it awkwardly, and shut it off.

"You guys... uh... I... that shouldn't have happened. I mean, that *couldn't have happened*? ...Why did that happen?" I softly said, sitting. Dumbfounded, I tried to decipher the impossible. My music app was not open, and even if it were, it would have returned to the former track I'd left it on, which wasn't this one. My iPhone was locked with a thumbprint ID to open it up, and I certainly hadn't had access to my thumbs while carrying the coffees.

I took short sips of breath, confused. I didn't want to be the center of attention, but somehow, something bigger than me had shoved me to the forefront. "I just don't know what it means?" I looked to the others for ideas.

Someone offered, "Maybe you should go to Jeri's room and play that Prince song?"

I sat on the suggestion for a second. Thoroughly perplexed, I rebutted, "I just can't imagine. The song starts getting overly energetic, talking about getting crazy and going nuts before we die."

We were all quiet, trying to solve the puzzle. There wasn't one of us who doubted the mystifying divinity of what had happened. I thought, maybe the message of "gathering here today to get through this thing called life" was what people needed to hear. At this point, the family had already resolved that Jeri wasn't going to make it.

"Do you think, maybe, just music in general?" Tammy said. "Maybe it wouldn't hurt just to have some music by her side?"

"Yeah, maybe," I affirmed. That wouldn't hurt, right? I was admittedly annoyed. If there was some divine presence offering up what was in our minds an absolute statistical impossibility, a miracle of sorts, could God not just plainly state what He or She wanted?

"Is it okay if I go back and sit with her a bit?" I looked at Tammy as I asked, but also included her dad in my gaze. Given that we were grasping at straws, we agreed that I'd go into Jeri's room and play a little music.

What a heartbreaking sight. I entered the room and saw Jeri incapacitated. There was a tube intubating her throat to help with her breathing, but surrounding the entry point to her mouth was blood, partially dried, partially wet, running down her chin.

"Is that normal?" I asked a nurse.

"It is," she replied. "She's on such a high level of blood thinners that the aggravation to her throat from the tube is expelling more blood than you would normally see."

I took a chair at Jeri's bedside, my eyes darting, familiarizing myself with all of the foreign wires, tubes, and machines that were helping her to hang on. My thoughts drifted to how traumatized Tammy must have been over the last few days, trying to make this environment her new normal, and whether it's even possible to normalize your child's suffering.

I folded my hands at Jeri's side. Given the confusing divine spark in the waiting room, it wasn't a question or wishful thinking as to whether God was listening. *God, I'm not sure what you're doing here, but please, show us your mercy. Please, help us find a way out of this.*

I pulled out my phone and cued up an album that I knew had a gentle, calming acoustic theme throughout. The guitars and ukulele softly filled the room.

It was almost immediate. I watched her hands move a little bit, signs that she had motor function. Her face contracted and winced, seemingly annoyed at the tube and the blood.

I let the music play and rested my hand near her arm to let her know she wasn't alone.

Tammy peeked around the folding glass entry. "She's moving?" Hope elevated in her sunken face.

"Yeah." I smiled. "She's doing something weird with her hands."

Tammy pulled a chair on the other side of the bed. "It's mom, love. I'm here, beautiful."

"Watch her hands." I tried not to speak too loudly.

We watched them for a bit. Tammy asked, "Is it sign language?"

We went to the nurse's station and asked if any of the nurses knew sign language. They sent us one.

"What is she doing. Is she trying to speak to us?" Tammy asked.

"I think she is." The nurse drew closer. "That's an H…O…W…S" she said, spelling out the words. "P-R-I-N-C-E. 'How's Prince?' Does that mean anything to you?"

"It does," Tammy said, laughing and crying with joy. "Prince is her two-year-old son."

Jeri was there. Her mind was there. Her motor skills were there. Her heart was there.

With a hopeful smile, I walked back into the waiting room, trying to get through a few positive words. My lack of sleep and conflicting emotions left my chin quivering, unable to speak. I signaled with my head to Jeri's sister and Dad that they should go back, and then I staggered to the outside of the hospital. I crossed my legs, sitting on the nearest patch of grass, cupping my eyes with the palms of my hands.

Within 24 hours, I had witnessed the worst of myself, my selfish brain chemistry and its desire to be fed above all else.

I had witnessed the fragility and the finality of life in the waiting room the night before.

But somehow, with all the selfishness and darkness looming over this whole circumstance, I had witnessed the divine and compassionate hand of God.

I wasn't certain whether I was ready to make changes with respect to my drinking, but I was now undoubtedly sure that if I were, then miraculous, otherworldly help was there for me.

I sat there by myself, pensive, pulling my hands from my soggy cheeks and recalling the chorus of the song I had played in Jeri's room:

I couldn't know…

How could I possibly have known…

We're not invincible

Slouched over, the emotional secret stirred within me: there were two of us dying in the ICU room that day.

◻˝F ß €ʳ◻

The mountain air drifted through the partially cracked window, filling our car's silence. I reached for Tammy's hand. "Hard not to think of Jeri when that album comes on, huh?"

"Seems like a lifetime ago," Tammy replied, still deep in thought. "Time stood still trying to get through that. It was such a miracle that she made it."

"Supernatural, for sure," I said. "I mean, we were rescued. The word grace sounds like a fluffy, Hallmark dream until you see it in action. We sat there, at our end with nothing to offer, no control, no solutions, and this grace sits alongside saying, 'Okay, now it's my turn.' We were in too much of a mess. We didn't even realize it was there. That's grace."

I could feel Tammy turn towards me. "And it wasn't just moving on Jeri's behalf, was it?"

Jeff Bowersox

Chapter 11

The Parking Lot

<u>5:25 PM</u>

Almost halfway home, our drive was fluid and easy. Unlike on our way to Bishop Castle, we knew where we were going now, so we moved through the muted tones of the landscape at a quicker pace than before.

We kept our music at a low volume as we feverishly discussed Bishop Castle, as if to not mention it was to risk letting it escape our memory forever. In part, we needed validation that what had started as a seed of an idea this morning had blossomed into a substantial day beyond our expectations. We talked about the decorative cement corner pieces that anchored portions of the exterior castle. There were the Taj Mahal-style caps on one of the towers that left us pontificating about how Jim Bishop went about fabricating them on his own.

Beyond detailing the visuals, we talked about Mr. Bishop's grit. I mentioned how I'd enjoyed the creativity of building our flagstone patio, but after two weeks of carrying rock, I was ready to golf for the rest of the summer. A lifetime of setting stones? Maybe when the nice lady at the gift shop talked about the castle coming with a lot of sacrifice, it wasn't just the loss of life; maybe it was the loss of time for other hobbies, as well? I joked that Jim Bishop's version of pornography was probably a centerfold of a bass fishing boat in a Cabela's catalogue.

All kidding aside, our conversation rested in utter amazement. We used words like *devotion*, *freedom*, *principled*, *artistic*, *determination*, and *inspiring*.

Tammy mused, "I'm so intrigued by Jim Bishop's history. I would have loved to have been a little birdie in the tree when a county official approached him and asked whether he had a permit. Did he rage? Did he laugh? Did he fire up his wood chipper and threaten to throw the guy in it?" She giggled. "I wonder if the county assessors ever tried to increase the property taxes because there was a dwelling on it. Don't you assess property taxes by comparing other 'like' dwellings in the area?"

"*Right?* Could you see the bean-counters trying to determine a value?" I continued in a deep, official voice, "Well, boss, the nearest thing I could find is this Greystone, mid-1700s three-level in Scotland." We laughed. "It's interesting how whenever you want to create or build something, there seems to be people in line trying to graft a portion from it, like, to take agency and gain a foothold in your process."

I sailed over a downward bend in the highway, more confident at a rapid speed. "I guess being sober, I found so many parallels today. I personally don't care if I'm required to get a permit to add a garage to our cabin, right? I mean, I've been conditioned to believe that someone out there is supposed to know better than I do. But today, I look at Jim Bishop and wonder, what if he would have given over agency to the officials? Would he have been bogged down or denied to the point of giving up? I could easily see that happening. So, like, I think about how it relates to alcohol. For me, I used to give over my agency every time I would drink. Drinking taxed my freedom. It took away all my power to create free-flowing experiences like we had today."

Then another feeling crept in. I thought of the minimal effort it should have taken me in previous years to just wake up in the early morning, pop into the car, and drive the two-plus hours to see Bishop Castle. I might have come away with what *real effort* and a sense of purpose looked like decades sooner. I felt ashamed that I had wasted so many years in allowing alcohol to steal my inspiration. I remained proud of the effort I had put into getting sober, but our drive home provided a generous amount of time for altering history. Taking a deep breath, I let my present freedom beat back regret.

"You wanna listen to a podcast?" I asked, noting a lapse in our conversation.

"Sure!" Her enthusiasm suggested that she agreed: something different would be nice.

I had a strong affection for podcasts. It wasn't just white noise or the need to have some filler in the background. These stories were my story. These people were my people: sober people. I had amassed a digital collection of friends who provided me my daily sustenance and encouragement when it was time to get sober. As I had approached the final freefall in my relationship with alcohol, it would be the stories on these podcasts that helped me realize that my struggle was not unique…

◌⸴F ℬ 𝒞⸴◌

I sat grooming the trampled grass outside of the hospital. I picked at it. I smoothed it over. Lost in its fibers and texture, I sat dumbstruck at what had just happened. It was almost impossible to sit with myself, having borne witness to so much hope, the goodness of it beating against my insides that were so trampled and defeated.

I felt the soft touch of Tammy's hand. She pulled up next to me, legs crossed, and leaned her head on my shoulder. Then we sobbed, uncontrollably, using each other for support as we emptied ourselves.

After a few minutes, I wiped my face with my sleeve and asked, "How's she doing?"

"She's there," Tammy said, nodding. "She's already bossing us around with her hands." Laughing and sniveling at the same time, she went on, "We have a whiteboard to write the letters down that she's signing, but we're not fast enough at guessing what she's saying. We're laughing like it's a game show and she's getting frustrated with us."

I laughed, taking another pass at my face with my palms.

"Are *you* okay?" Tammy dipped her head to look at me, letting me know that she had time for an honest answer. She wiggled my knee playfully. "Channeling Prince and God all in the same morning looks like exhausting work. Big shoes to fill, eh?"

I paused. I debated inside my head, between speaking my truth and adding more to Tammy's worry, versus just holding off for a while.

"Honestly, I don't know if I'm okay. I mean… No, I'm not okay at all." I wasn't sure if I had the intellectual capacity, or even the slightest understanding of what I was feeling, to be able to relay it to her.

I kept it vague. "I don't know, it's just… this whole thing. This whole experience has left me wanting to make some changes. It's testing what I value and where my allegiances are. I mean *that…*" I sharply pointed towards the hospital doors. "What happened in *there*? There must be a higher calling in life than me just dulling every moment with alcohol. I think back to when I was in my car accident, and I put my parents and Nathan through what we just went through? I can hardly sit with myself, I feel such regret."

Tammy remained close. She listened. I was so thankful to have a friend and a partner that I could be honest with, but at the same time, my stubborn, people-pleasing nature had me questioning whether this was the best time for me to be offloading my issues onto her. It seemed selfish. I let the silence be my guide. I didn't want to offer any commitments to quit drinking, and I certainly didn't want to burden her with having to watch over me during withdrawal. Nevertheless, I rested in knowing that I was able to put words to the inner battle that was warring for my future.

I continued with a tone that tried to assure Tammy that we were winding down my issues. "I don't know what this is, why alcohol is so important. I should want to be fully in the moment, but all I really want to do is escape. I want to turn it off, my brain... I just want to turn off my thoughts."

"I understand, love. Believe me, I do." She gently rubbed my forearm. "Who wouldn't want to remove themselves from all this pain and confusion? I think we're going to get through this. We'll get everything back to normal."

My addict brain immediately recognized a glimmer of hope in her words: *back to normal.* Of course, it identified *normal* as being our freedom to drink daily, just as we were doing a week ago. I lifted from my slump, disturbingly satisfied that my vague description had seemed to extend only to our present circumstance. I hadn't been honest about how debilitating the disease was becoming, about my growing mental obsession, or about the ways I had been sneakily increasing my intake during our *normal* times.

My miraculous moment of clarity had already begun getting levied by partial truths.

Jeri had been in the hospital for the better part of two weeks. She spent her time undergoing CAT scans, MRIs, and numerous rehabilitative and monitoring procedures. The doctors agreed that she could leave the hospital, but only under 24-hour supervision. There was uncertainty as to whether the blood clotting issue would resurface, thus needing her to be entirely in someone else's care.

Tammy insisted that Jeri come home with us. Our mountain home was not ideal if an emergency arose, but what it lacked in space and convenience, it made up for with Tammy's devoted care.

That fall season wasn't ideal for what Tammy and I had designed as our *normal*. Drinking for me was only part of the equation. I'd like to say it was because God parted the Red Sea in the hospital room that day, that the scales fell from my eyes and I was miraculously launched into a life of sobriety. But I wasn't.

Jeri moved in with us, and it was almost impossible to drink with any degree of certainty that we wouldn't have an emergency that forced us back into town. My alcohol consumption was partially paralyzed by a greater fear of needing to be responsible at a moment's notice. I was white-knuckling a sobriety where I had not even drawn a line in the sand and made a full commitment to not drinking. Instead of viewing my circumstances as a blessing in disguise, Jeri living with us triggered an undercurrent of resentment that I wasn't free to drink.

How was it that, after all this time, I still associated drinking with freedom?

Those seemingly harmless first drinks with the neighbors, well over a decade ago, showed that *I wasn't free* to commune and have meaningful conversations without loosening the guard of my insecurities.

The growing discontent of the unequal responsibilities in my first marriage showed that alcohol didn't *free me* to honestly interact in a restorative way; it allowed me to hide and bury my truths.

A DUI, received after deciding to take the responsibility upon myself to get our neighbors home from the bar, showed that *I wasn't free* to make clear decisions, allowing my people-pleasing nature to run on steroids. *I wasn't free* to return to my exceptional genetic research career. *I wasn't free* to process the pain of infidelity. *I wasn't free* to wipe my own ass after a near-death car accident. *I wasn't free* to stare my friends in the face after missing their wedding. *I wasn't free* to take my son to UFC Fight Night, because I had been locked in jail on the rare night it was held in Denver. *I wasn't free* to operate my business without a driver. *I wasn't free* to support my wife in her most frightening and crippling crisis.

Freedom to drink wasn't freedom; it took, and it continued to take. It took my confidence. It took my time. It took my mind. It took my mobility. It took my health. This was the opposite of freedom, and yet I let it continue even as I started to recognize what it was doing to me.

As I stepped over Jeri's legs propped on the ottoman in the living room, I peered up above the fridge to where the vodka rested, unopened. I was well aware that I was never fully present. Instead, I gazed into the future, longing to resume my alcohol use. Stringing together weeks at a time without drinking gave me again the false confidence that I was okay, allowing me to ignore all my history to the contrary.

After several months of affirming follow-up doctor's visits, Jeri returned to her apartment, on the condition that her roommate continued to monitor her less restricted care. Our small cabin embraced just the two of us once again, returning our lives towards each other, lessening critical responsibilities. We lounged on the sofa, Tammy tucking her head into the socket of my chest and bicep. She played on her phone, scrolling Facebook, while I concentrated on the sounds of late autumn slipping through our partially cracked window.

"It looks like they're a having a birthday get-together for Andy at the Sprucewood on Saturday," Tammy said.

"Yeah?" My chin dipped as I peeked at her phone.

Tammy had never quite dismissed our conversation on the grass outside of the hospital. Even though I had been vague, she seemed to understand that it was a defining moment for me in curbing my alcohol use. Even if I cut back to minimal drinking, it was forever impossible to view the outside world as being responsible for what I now knew was internal. My forced quitting, precipitated by Jeri's occupation of our space and time, appeared more definitive to Tammy than I'd wanted it to be. For Tammy, not being inside my mind, not having my issues, I wondered if she had any clue that my putting down the bottle for that brief amount of time, carried the amount of agitation and distress that it did. I was constantly tarrying whether my decision had to be final. I had not completely resolved that I was a non-drinker. It seemed impossible to approach festive events without imbibing like everybody else.

"It'll be okay if we drink at Andy's party, don't you think?" I asked.

"How do you feel about it?" Tammy was looking for me to be the judge of my own court.

"Well, I mean, it's a party, right? I feel pretty strong in how I've abstained over the last few months." I eased into expanding the parameters. "I think we should be allowed to have a weekend now and again where we let go."

The party wasn't until Saturday, but I had managed to broaden the window for a weekend of drinking. Relief pulsed through me as I drove home

Thursday night, spirits in tow, all of my work having been cleared until Sunday afternoon. I had stopped at the liquor store, ceremoniously parading around the beer and vodka section, making sure to get more than enough for a full weekend.

Using a familiar justification in my playbook, I had convinced myself that, since I worked on Sunday, this meant Thursday was my Friday. It was something I had done countless times before. Necking back that first beer on Thursday night immediately fired every synapse that had been lying dormant over the past few months. Whatever death grip I'd had over moderation succumbed to the time and opportunity I had carved out for myself.

My Thursday bled into the wee hours of Friday morning. It was almost premeditated; the longer I stayed up, the more likely it was that I would sleep most of Friday, thereby rolling right into the evening hour when it was more acceptable to continue drinking. With my stomach unsettled from the previous night, I made light grilled salmon with an Asian slaw salad for dinner, and Tammy and I treated it more like a proper drinking night. A crisp vodka and tonic with lime slid down quickly along with the light entrees.

I glided off the couch to stoke the fireplace, collecting our glasses to refill our spirits. We bantered about the Christmas shopping that we had accomplished in the previous week. Music bounced off the knotty pine siding in our family room. I was flushed by the warmth of confidence as I belted out songs during our card games. This was the *us* I loved, the sweet spot where I wanted to be. I wanted Tammy by my side, all to myself, and I wanted the limitless burn of each sip of alcohol reminding me that the outside world couldn't burden us for a while.

Saturday, prior to Andy's birthday party, gave way to hidden day drinking. The uncomfortable nausea I woke up with on Saturday was easily placated by a morning nip of vodka. I kept myself slightly buzzed throughout the day, so as not to get sick, and then primed myself a little stronger just before we headed down the dirt road to our friend's birthday celebration.

This experience didn't culminate in some fantastical rock bottom moment that trumped all of my former embarrassments. At least, I don't think it did. I couldn't remember the party. I couldn't remember anything. Blank. *A blackout?* I spent Thursday through Saturday feeding the hungry ghost that crouched beneath my hollow shell and woke up sometime on Sunday watching football in the family room with Nathan and Tammy.

Somehow, I had lost time. The disorienting feeling of looking around our family room, trying to gain clues and recollect whether I had done anything wrong, was eased by the familiar atmosphere. I looked at Tammy, searching for a safety in her presence. She smiled. "Good morning."

Nathan chirped from the kitchen table, "Morning, honey."

It wasn't morning; it was the afternoon, but the playful greetings eased me from the fear that my carved-out memory had prompted.

Deception from an addict is simple. "What time do you think we got home last night?"

I knew that Tammy would start filling in the details, so I wouldn't need to ask any more questions that betrayed that my memory was completely wiped.

"Probably around 1:30," she said. "You were so tired, you hit the couch and were out before I could get my makeup off. It was so good seeing everyone."

Another reprieve. Phew. It seemed like a casual ending. *No aggression. No weird arguments.*

I peered towards the table. My wallet, keys, and phone were neatly stacked. *Nothing lost.*

I scanned the kitchen counter. The bottle of vodka had the same level as it did before we'd left for the Sprucewood. *I didn't drink more when I came home.*

For an addict, deception is simple. "I slept hard. I wonder if I'm coming down with something?"

Sitting there watching football, I felt sour. This brought back my memory of the handheld breathalyzer and interlock device on my car, the foggy feeling of waking up and being too drunk to pass the test. I hadn't drunk anything since we got home from the party, but I was certain that after a combined 10 hours of sleep and watching football that my throbbing liver had still not processed the alcohol.

The Broncos were playing poorly and had just eliminated its chances of getting into the playoffs. I used the players' poor performance as a deceptive excuse for my gruff disposition and pre-hungover state. Convincing myself that my blood alcohol content was dwindling, I headed to work to expel my handful of evening duties. I didn't want to finish watching the game with Tammy and Nathan for fear that, in such close quarters, they might see my hands starting to shake.

Driving down the mountain road that Sunday evening was surreal. I kept clinching my eyelids shut a brief moment longer than a standard blink, trying to trick my brain into adjusting the blur. As I edged closer to town, I lost all confidence that I wasn't under the influence. My slow, cautious drive afforded me uninvited time for contemplation... *Why can't I just be like everyone else? I've been drinking since Thursday night... Why can't I stop this? Why do I keep messing up my chance to be normal?*

Slightly relieved, slightly trembling, I pulled into the parking lot of my business. I sat... and I sat.

I sat there searching for the answer to an unsolvable equation. With my soggy brain fashioning what I thought was a good idea, I strongly considered driving myself to the police station so they could test me. If I remained hot with alcohol in my system, they could put me in jail for the mandatory one year... *I would be free then... In jail, I would be free.*

I thought about that solution long enough to scare myself. Madness. Instead, I chose to just get to work. Moving around would help me metabolize and take my mind off of making nonsensical decisions.

I only had to work for a few hours, and on the way home, I found myself even more contemplative than when I had arrived.

I was disgusted at the paradox that prior to this three-day bender, I was driving home Thursday night with such blissful anticipation for the weekend ahead. The false promises of alcohol elicited thoughts of fun and vitality, yet left me three days later with my mind, body, and spirit lacking both. I didn't have all the environmental excuses that I used to carry; I had nothing to blame for my insatiable use of alcohol. In the past, if I had made a mistake in drinking too much, I would think, "Yeah, that was a stupid thing to do." The *action* was stupid… The *thing* that I did was stupid.

Now, my hatred had become internalized. *I am stupid.*

I was fully engulfed by the shame of addiction. I didn't *do* a stupid thing… I *was* this stupid thing.

Shame is a horrible imprisonment. I felt unworthy of any goodness that had unfolded past my former drinking mistakes. I needed to self-punish to rectify the defect that was inside of me.

It made sense, then, why I would consider driving to the police station and having them lock me up. It made sense that I would find more peace in jail than I ever would trying to navigate the complexity of my fucked up brain.

I had reached the final stretch of paved road, less than a mile from home. The desperation in my mind was like a pinball machine trying to regulate chaos into order. I didn't have any answers, but I was sincerely trying to figure it out. I kept picturing the absurdity of me sitting in that parking lot, ready to give myself to the police, ready to turn myself in and surrender.

A simple, but revelatory thought occurred to me: to consider driving to the police station would be an act that said, *I can't control alcohol by myself. I need help.*

That's all it was. The grand epiphany was that I considered reaching out for help. By considering giving myself to a more empowered authority, I was saying, "I *need* help. I *need* something bigger and more powerful than myself to help me."

I pulled onto our dirt driveway, quietly shutting off the car and turning down the lights, wanting more time to sort my thoughts. I wasn't ready to ask for help. Somehow, this seemed like a white flag that undermined my ego-driven notion that I could do it all, that I could manage it all.

I hated feeling vulnerable. I hated the idea of anybody thinking of me as weak or less-than. My whole adulthood was armored with these flimsy tools of pride, people-pleasing, and the outward illusion that I can handle everything.

I sat there in the driveway and I thought of Tammy. I played back the tape, visions of her kissing my face when I'd let my guard down, unveiling my frailty, my imperfections. How moments of untethered, raw honesty had always delivered liberation. How she loved me for who I was, exactly where I was at. My truth would be safe with her. I realized that I was letting alcohol chip away at the virtue that I valued most between us, the very foundation of our relationship: *honesty*.

I had promised Tammy that I would always be honest, no matter what, and maybe the creeping shame filling my insides wasn't just from the lack of control I had over alcohol, but also from the betrayal of my commitment to let her share my struggles. I could trust her with this. She had always been worthy of my trust.

With one hand holding my car keys and the other massaging my temples, I felt forced to plan an action that I would stick with. Pragmatically, I wouldn't be able to abstain from drinking tonight. My insides were giving me all the warning signs of uncomfortable withdrawals. I would quit tomorrow. I would tell Tammy everything tomorrow.

Walking up our dirt driveway towards the cabin, fallen pine needles crunching under each step, the final approach to our home felt surreal, a perp walk heading towards surrender. I walked through the front patio that adjoined our kitchen, peering through the sliding glass door towards the living room. Tammy and Nathan sat in the family room, laughing at the TV.

In full view, I walked steadfastly into the kitchen. I didn't wait for someone to leave their vantage point of me and I didn't angle my body as a shield while I made a drink. I grabbed the half-full vodka bottle, poured a shot into a tumbler glass, and slid it down my throat. Then I poured two inches more and added some ice.

As I walked towards the sofa, Tammy's mouth half-dropped, delivering a frightened look of deep concern. I had my barren, needy dependence on full display. The honesty began; they had to see what desperation and lack of control looked like.

As Nathan got up to get ready for bed, I stared stoically at the TV. I gripped the drink in my hand, knowing for certain that tomorrow it would come to an end.

"Love?" Tammy whispered. "Are you okay? What's wrong?"

I stared at her. I just shook my head, I looked down at my glass and just continued to shake my head. "Can we talk about this tomorrow? I do really need to talk to you."

"Do you want to talk now? You're scaring me a little."

"I can't now. I just can't. Please... It needs to be tomorrow."

She seemed to sense that my tone was sincere.

"G'night, Dad... Love you!" Nathan said as he passed from the bathroom to the bedroom.

I mustered a half-smile. "Love you, buddy."

"I'm going to get ready for bed," Tammy said, getting up. "See you in there?"

"Yeah," I said with the same forced smile. "I'll be in in a bit."

I turned the TV off and stared at my glass. I was full of fear. In my decade-plus-long relationship with alcohol, I had never said goodbye on my own terms; it had never been my decision. I'd had consequences that littered my history with forced reasons to stop, but never once had I come to some internal understanding that I had to make the choice.

I gulped the straight cocktail down and stepped back into the kitchen. I knew I would need four or five drinks in my system to help me sleep until the morning, when I would follow through with my decision to tell Tammy everything. If I didn't have the medicine inside me, I would lie awake shaking, thinking, and I didn't trust myself in the middle of the night alone with my thoughts.

I tilted the half-full bottle into my glass one last time, and then carefully capped it. I was deflated, sick and tired of feeling sick and tired. I threw the final shots down my throat and set my glass in the sink with zero feelings of fanfare or nostalgia. It was simply a means to an end, and this was the end.

I braced myself against the edge of the counter, leaned over, and pressed my forehead to the cap of the bottle. We weren't negotiating anymore. The reality was cemented; yes, I had overcome my former drinking consequences, but the final consequence would be death, a permanent penalty I could not manipulate. I pressed my forehead harder into the bottle cap, picturing the barrel of a gun. My teeth clenched; a tear squeezed out through my eyelids. I whispered, "It's either me or you… and it's not going to be me." I stood up, took a deep breath, and pushed the bottle next to the coffee machine.

Leaving the kitchen without turning back, I said out loud, "I'm done."

Chapter 12

The Patio

6:45 PM

The Colorado foothills opened to reveal the familiar sprawl of civilization. The lights of the expansive suburbs dotted the darkness of the landscape. We were a full hour into our podcast and making excellent time getting back to town.

"We're about 20 minutes from home," I said. "Should we stop somewhere and eat?"

"Heck yeah," Tammy said. "Maybe the Speedtrap? Do they stay open for dinner?"

"That sounds *really* good. Let's swing by and see"

We were listening to The Armchair Expert podcast, co-hosted by actor Dax Shepard, who was 14 years sober at the time. Over our Jeep's audio system,

Dax told his guest, "It's easier to act your way into changing your thinking, than to think your way into changing your actions."

"You know," I said, "I still have this childlike electricity flowing through me. Today seemed profound on so many levels."

"How do you mean?"

"Well, like, what he just said. 'It's easier to act your way into changing your thinking, than to think your way into changing your actions.' I keep thinking about Jim Bishop. He didn't know he was going to build this grand castle where everyone would start to hear about it and come visit. He didn't know. *He couldn't have known.* He didn't think his way into building that castle. There were no blueprints. He just showed up on the first day and started laying rocks. He thought it was going to be this small cottage, but it turned into this beautifully unique project."

Tammy said, "I can see that. Like, if you would have told him on Day 1 that he'd spend 50 years building a castle, with no blueprints, no permits or instructions, and he'd end up inspiring tens of thousands of people along the way, he probably would have panicked and never started."

"And those being the triumphs," I added. "If you told him there would be perpetual struggle with the government and the loss of a child? You'd be overwhelmed if all the hardships and uncertainties were right before you all at once. You couldn't think your way through all of it. But instead, he just showed up every day and put it into action.

"And that's why I say that today seems profound. The whole thing seems so connected with recovery and staying sober. I had no idea we would be here 21 months ago. I couldn't *think* my way into a better future, what it would look like. I was a mess. I was terrified the day I told you I needed your help to quit drinking. I was so scared that I would be this bland, sacrificial martyr that was only quitting to make everyone else happy. I just figured I was trading the freedom in drinking for a few more years of my miserable life. It didn't seem appealing, cutting myself out of fun events and not being able to drink like other people. It's why I held on so long, why I didn't quit sooner. But I never dreamed I could feel the way I do now, so confident and at peace, let alone that I'd have the freedom to go on adventures like this. It's like the castle—there's this glorious thing building in me, and I never would have guessed that in the beginning."

Tammy added with a smile, "I can see where you draw the similarities. You started laying the foundation, not knowing what it would turn into. You just woke up on that first day and got started."

□˝F 𝕭 €˝□

Alcohol withdrawal starts with simply waking up. Contrary to your body needing rest from the poison, your brain wakes you up and alerts you that it is unsatisfied, that it needs more.

My first day of recovery started with a contradiction; I wanted to feel well, but the easiest solution was to answer to my scrambled brain chemistry. This might be the most important distinction for a person prone to alcoholism versus a normal drinker: if a normal drinker has a little too much, their body tells them that they are in danger if they do it again, and they easily heed the warning; when a person with alcohol dependence drinks too much, his mind convinces him that to continue killing himself is the means for survival.

I had purposely set the bottle of vodka next to the coffee maker the night before. As I woke up and moved towards the kitchen, I could feel the anxious shortening of breath in my chest. Depression-filled tears started to well up in my eyes as I stood at the kitchen counter, about to make the first of what I thought would be a million more oppressive choices to not drink in the future. I had heard of alcoholics who poured everything down the sink so that they wouldn't have any alcohol within their reach when quitting, but that didn't make sense to me. Booze would always be there, whether it was on my counter, in my cupboard, down the street at the bar, or 20 minutes away on a grocery store shelf. Even on Day 1, I felt like I had to stare down that realization. Whether or not I drank would forever be a conscious choice; it wouldn't be because I tripped and fell into an open bottle that happened to be nearby.

I reached under the cabinet and slid the coffee maker out, leaving the vodka where it was. I quietly prepared the coffee, relieved that Tammy was still asleep. My mental fog was thick, and the fear of not knowing how to explain to Tammy that I needed to quit drinking for good would be buffered by some time alone with my thoughts.

I took my coffee out to our window-enclosed patio, which overhung the crisp mountain property. It seemed that with every introspective second, I was overwhelmed with fear, afraid to accept what I knew was true. *This patio. We've had so many fun, alcohol-fueled moments on this patio. This is where we popped champagne and signed our wedding certificate, right here. Is life going to be dull now, bland…? What will we do?*

I sat, crossing my leg over my knee, staring through the giant trees, and trying to draw some type of comfort from a future I could not foresee. I predicted a jail sentence of boredom. I remembered friends coming up to camp for the weekend, not here 10 minutes before their beer coolers sprung from the backseat. *Would friends still want to come up and hang out if they knew I wasn't drinking? Will I lose more friends?*

I watched steam rise from my coffee as the frigid December air bit through the patio windows. My hands shook. I didn't know if my tremors were because of the temperature or because my withdrawals were about to begin, but it didn't matter; the shakes would come. I thought that if I was shaking from the weather, maybe it would satisfy my desire to not worry Tammy. I wouldn't have to explain how quickly a four-day bender had developed into dependence. I sighed, shaking my head, recognizing that I was already leaning towards harm reduction, trying to minimize her concern. *Honesty*, I reminded myself. *When I sat outside in the car last night, I had resolved to be completely honest.*

But I wasn't sure how to be honest. Maybe I could be completely honest if I knew how to completely explain what was wrong. I couldn't, though. I didn't understand why I'd been able to casually partake in drinking events in my twenties without any propensity towards addiction or lack of control. I could explain the alcohol abuse around the time of my divorce; external circumstances were my reasoning for that. *But now...* I couldn't explain what was wrong with me *now*. I loved my life. I loved our present time. There was no other place I'd rather be, and...

"Jeff?" Tammy called from the kitchen.

"I'm out here, love," I answered.

She came out with her own cup of coffee nestled in her hands. "Hey," she whispered, as if recognizing my need to feel safe.

My eyes were swollen, and I bit my lower lip, not certain if I was ready.

She pulled up the chair next to me, warm but deeply concerned. "Can you tell me what's going on? I'm really worried. Is it us?"

"Oh, love, no… God, no. It's not us. It's me… There's something wrong with *me.*"

I returned my stare out the window and paused. I took a deep breath, not knowing how or where to start. Without movement, a statue lacking any theatrics, tears wetted my cheekbones; *I surrendered.*

"I'm sick. I don't know how to explain it really, but there's something wrong inside my head. I… I can't drink anymore. I don't want to drink anymore. Not even a little."

I didn't look to Tammy for a response. I stared concretely out the window, stunned that I had finally put words to my affliction. I continued, "Before this weekend, alcohol was all I could think about, knowing we would get to have some. It took over my daily thoughts, time that I could have used to think of other things, good things. And once we started drinking, I couldn't stop. I didn't want to stop. My mental obsession with alcohol is stronger than my will to do what's right. Something is broken… I just feel broken inside and I don't want to be like this anymore."

Tammy watched me as I spoke, listening quietly. "Can I ask," she said carefully, "did something happen last night at work? You came home different, like… You seemed like you'd gotten into some sort of trouble."

"Well…" I tried to figure out how to explain it. "I didn't *get* into any trouble… I guess I finally accepted that I *already was* in trouble. Last night, I felt like I might have been driving with alcohol in my system, and I realized that I just don't have any control over this thing. My answer to not having control was to drive myself to the police station. I didn't, but I wanted to. I wanted someone to help me, even force me, to control what I can't seem to manage on my own. I guess that's when I realized that I needed to ask you for help. If I was willing to put myself in the hands of strangers, I figured I should first try to put myself in the care of someone who actually loves me. You've always been worthy of my trust…

"…I'm sorry." I looked at her for the first time. "I've been dishonest. I've been deceiving you, trying to make it seem like my drinking's been okay. But it's not okay… I'm not okay. Far from it. The contradiction of what I show on the outside versus what I feel on the inside is eating me alive. The alcohol is physically and mentally eating me up. My joy and my interest in the future has been eaten up. I'm just getting devoured on all sides and I don't know how to stop it."

Tammy pulled her chair closer to mine. I slouched over, my hands massaging my temples. I felt her hand gently rub my shoulder and back. "We can stop it together, Jeff. We can do this together. I've often wondered if we weren't squandering valuable time. We can fill our time with better things. *We don't need it.*"

I mustered a barely perceptible nod. I didn't have the energy to smile and fake through what felt like defeat. "But what if we *do need it*? I don't… I can't stand the thought that… What if our relationship was built on some sort of need to manipulate our feelings or our environment? I'm so attached to our fun being intertwined with drinking. What if I'm boring... Angry... Not joyful or funny? I'm scared, Tammy. What if you don't like who I am? What if I don't like who we are without alcohol?"

Tammy leaned in. "So," she said, "do you like who you are right now? In this moment?"

"I don't," I said instantly. "I fucking hate this. I hate feeling like I'm wasting every good thing that's been put in front of me." I paused, dialing in the will to fully unload my truth. "Alcohol, the freedom to drink it, emboldens me, makes me feel like some type of renegade who's giving the system the middle finger. Like, I've beaten all the circumstances and authorities that have tried to suppress my drinking or tell me what to do. And on most days, and I get it, it's probably a delusion, but I feel like I've outsmarted them. I've been able to use beyond the warning signs and have still salvaged a great life. I have you... I love you. I have Nathan... He's still well parented, on point to do amazing things. We have friends and a home... I'm not living in a gutter somewhere filing for bankruptcy. It's just..."

Tammy and I sat in silence for a few moments. She continued to stroke my back, letting me come to my own thoughts in their time.

"It's just... I... We've created this beautiful world and it still doesn't work. If I managed to go through all that shit—the accident, the DUIs, disappointing friends and family... If I managed to survive and overcome that, rebuild a great life, and I'm *still* accelerating my drinking… The only thing that's going to stop me is death." I paused, settling on a firm truth. *"And I don't want to die…"*

"Maybe it's just my pride, but I don't want everyone standing over my hospital bed or graveside saying, 'That Jeff… he was a great guy. It's a shame he just couldn't figure out the drinking thing.'

"And I guess that's just it… *I can't* figure out the drinking thing." I lifted my head. All reservations broke into a full cry. "And I'm sorry, I don't want to be a burden, and I don't want to put the fear of the unknowns into our future, but I don't think there is a future if I don't get some help."

"Jeff, I'm excited." She leaned closer. "I am *truly* excited. We can make a list of hobbies, different things to do with our time. Remember when we first met? The courts wouldn't let you drink, and we had wonderful times! We went to the gym and you would goof off on the chin-up bars like a monkey. You smiled more during the day, sang, whistled… That person is in there." She placed her hand on my heart. "Everything I love about you is in there."

I emitted an exhausted sigh of relief as I tried to absorb Tammy's words. We let the silence rest, sipping our coffee.

I had been overwhelmed by the visitation of grace in Jeri's hospital room a few months ago, a gentle moment of clarity that prompted my stubborn alcohol use to change its course.

Now I sat in a state of open vulnerability, exposed, and in this moment of brokenness and surrender, I experienced empathy and mercy beyond what I felt I deserved.

I couldn't see into the future like Tammy. She saw it for me. I couldn't see how I'd make it past that day, but I did know that I had taken a step that I never had before… I'd been painstakingly honest about a defect that I'd known was growing for some time: I couldn't drink.

I gazed into an uncertain future, unsure if love, vitality, fun, and acceptance would survive in a realm of sobriety. I buried my soggy eyes in the flesh of Tammy's arm. I accepted it. "I'm sorry," I sobbed.

In that moment, my shame lifted. In that moment, I began to heal.

◦˝F ₿ €˝◦

As we exited the interstate toward the Speedtrap Bistro, I was already mentally eyeing the menu, even though I had all but settled on my favorite—ham and swiss crepes with asparagus.

"I can't wait to look at the pictures," Tammy said, breaking through my drifting thoughts.

"We took quite a few, huh? It was all so unique, you wanted to capture all the details. You probably wouldn't believe any of it if you didn't see it again."

"What was your favorite part?" she asked.

"Of the castle?"

"Of any of it… Of the whole day?"

"Hmmmm." I stalled for time. "That's an impossible question. Honestly, the best part is how I feel right now. This moment is the best part, knowing that this day happened at all. I feel like we were really out there living today. We were impulsive, active, carefree. We just got to be us, and I love us."

I gave Tammy's leg an assuring squeeze, then added, "I don't know, like, beyond just the eccentric adventure of it all, I have this emboldened understanding of integrity. I feel like all those years I was drinking, I postured like I had these virtues and principles, but drinking somehow corroded them or had me hiding because I couldn't live up to them. Like I was divided or broken or something. I don't feel that anymore… I don't feel divided. My insides match my outsides. It doesn't make me feel proud, or even better than I was. I just feel whole, like, I'm not missing anything. There was something about Jim Bishop and his castle… I dunno, there was all this visual affirmation of what can be accomplished when you apply your principles and a lot of grit. But also… So, Jim Bishop knew that if he let some external authority get a stranglehold, it would stifle his ability to create the world he wanted. I think about that metaphorically. With alcohol, for me, it's like, to drink is to give up my agency. To let something else hijack my future. I guess today felt like freedom," I said. "True freedom."

The parking lot was busier than I expected. As we hopped out and approached the bistro's door, I asked, "What was your favorite part of the day?"

Tammy soured her face playfully like it went without needing to ask. I opened the door for her, and she poked me as she walked through. "The dungeon, silly... My favorite part was the dungeon."

Epilogue

7:20PM

Hanging up the phone with Nathan, I stepped back inside the small bistro.

Tammy sat at a table in the distance, already swiping through the pictures on her phone while she nursed her cocktail. I was greeted by her giant grin and a steaming cup of black coffee in front of my seat.

"How's Nathan?" Tammy asked.

"Well," I said, "I think I scared him into thinking we joined a cult?"

"What?" Tammy chuckled. "Why would he think that?"

I slipped into my seat and took a gentle tester of my coffee. "Oh, I dunno," I said, sarcastically. "I told him we traveled deep into the San Isabel National Forest and met a five-foot-tall, 75-year-old man who built a giant castle by himself. I think I may have sounded overly giddy. He asked if we had joined a cult."

Tammy and I doubled over in laughter. "That's hilarious," she said. "It *does* sound a little culty."

We nestled up shoulder to shoulder, swiping through the images. We recounted the old pickup truck, the castle towers looming above the tree line, the warning signs, and a lot of close-ups of the detailed architecture. I'd find a fantastic picture and push my phone in Tammy's direction, and she'd do the same.

As Tammy found a funny picture of me frightened and easing my way out on the iron bridge wobbling in the sky, she caught me staring into the nothingness of the restaurant's ceiling.

"Hey?" Tammy eased her phone back from my view. "You okay?"

I tried to shake the thought, not wanting to spoil the mood, but I could already feel the tears rising.

"Jeff? Hey. What are you thinking about?" She put her hand on my forearm.

I adjusted my head towards the table, fumbling with my phone. Maybe the biggest difference in sobriety is that I now need to receive and process my feelings, instead of simply burying them.

"Well." I spoke slowly, trying to keep my emotions from bursting. "I guess I was just thinking, of all the pictures we do have, I wish I had the one that was never taken. Remember when I took the picture of that father and his little boy next to Jim Bishop?"

Tammy nodded. "I do."

"I just had the thought, that could have been Nathan and me. You know, like, over ten years ago, that could have been us. I just... The thought that I let my drinking steal any beautiful moments like we had today, rattles me a little." I quickly swiped my cheek, trying to contain myself.

Tammy leaned in. "Yeah, but you know what? Your recovery has created today, and hundreds if not thousands more days like it in the future. You'll forever use the day we found Bishop Castle as a reminder to create more days like it, days with Nathan and with our family, days that you couldn't have imagined were possible on Day 1."

Nodding, knowing I couldn't live in regret, I took a deep breath and received her wisdom.

Two musicians clunked their guitar cases through the front door of the busy café, already buzzing with people.

Ever my support and always my friend, Tammy said, "You know, it's going to be weird; these musicians are going to set up and we'll be about to leave. It might look rude. Do you want to leave now and go eat somewhere that's quieter?"

I sighed and nodded, accepting her rescue.

Surveying our table, I asked, "Don't you want to finish your drink first?"

"No, not at all," Tammy said casually. "I don't need it."

I stood up and slid a twenty in between my coffee and her cocktail. "Yeah," I said, brimming with the day's victory, "neither do I."

The End

Beyond Bishop Castle: My Recovery

Thank you for traveling with me through *Finding Bishop Castle*. To discover how I went from day-one to day-awesome, please join me at OurAfterglow.com for a humorous, free 4-part bonus supplement that details key fundamentals in my recovery.

OurAfterglow.com is an inclusive collective that celebrates all forms of recovery. You will find the important, but oft ignored, element that we should all incorporate into our programs: fun!

I am committed to encouraging, cultivating, and promoting stories like *Finding Bishop Castle*, and making them a reality in your own life. If you are struggling with alcohol or substance abuse, please join me. If you have put the acute pain of addiction in your rearview, come alongside me so that we can elevate each other's joy in what lies ahead.

OurAfterglow.com… because the recovery community could use a "fun uncle."

Acknowledgments

Without exception, I'd first like to say thank you to Tammy. You are my heart. It's altogether different to theorize about the concept of grace versus receiving it from a living, breathing human being. You opened a door to my soul that I thought might forever be shut. Thank you for taking this ride with me... Forever.

Nathan, thank you. Buddy, all we ask is that our children end up as better versions of ourselves. Your intelligence, thoughtfulness, and resilience are already measuring beyond what we could have hoped for. I continue with you, not as a dad, but as a friend. For that, I am grateful.

To my family, thank you for patiently sticking with me. Thank you for never being harder on me than I was being on myself.

To Natasha, thank you for getting the ball rolling again. Your tears in what was probably a coarse first version was fuel to finish developing this for the rest of the world. I was content to put it down and leave it as my story. You reminded me that it's *our story*.

To Tricia Lewis, you traveled a couple weeks ahead of me on this recovery journey and you did it like a person with a machete clearing a trail in the Guyana jungle. With all that vigor, you never forgot to reach back a hand to see if we were coming along. Your genuine sincerity in this sober movement is unmatched, your authenticity, my measuring stick.

To my relentless editor, Elizabeth Jahns, thank you for exacting your expertise and executing it with tedious precision (I left that string of $5 words as an inside joke because you are worth every one of them). You took the music in my head and helped me sound like I can carry a tune. I've got some more songs. We will partner again...

To Maren, I was limited in day's journey to time stamp through events that actually happened. If I could fabricate a moment, I would have added a bridge. A single chapter, though, wouldn't do justice in recording the light you shed on time wasted versus time well spent. The love and kindness you shared with me will always be remembered as critical bridge in my recognizing the need heal.

To the Recovery Elevator Podcast, Paul Churchill, Odette, and the administrative team: Your platform took a broken, desperate, 41-year-old man, crying on his front patio, and instantly put hope in his hands. You saved my life. Period.

To Café RE OG, thank you. At any moment, at any time, anywhere in the world, you can help me, and I can help you. It works; we are all proof. Thanks specifically to Natasha, Matt, Kate, Hilary, Scott, Sherrie, Blair, Amy, and Chris for early feedback on the manuscript. If I forgot anyone, please forgive me. You are all essential!

Thank you to Dax Shepard, Monica Padman, Justin Furstenfeld, Rob Bell, Brené Brown, and Pete Holmes. Your creativity and art has led me well past the symptom of alcoholism and into overall better mental health.

Thank you to my Sober as SH*T Facebook family. I've recovered along with thousands of people, and to do that takes honesty and vulnerability. When you find a select few that can provide that safety while casually inserting dick jokes, that's being back at the bar without the poison. You've been the closest of friends, providing undying support.

To Allison, we love you. You shine. You shine for us when we can't see the shimmer in ourselves. Let's sparkle on...

Lastly, to Mr. Jim Bishop: When I want to give up, I think... *move one more boulder*. When I am uncertain of my purpose, I imagine... *just bend this piece of iron*. Thank you for reminding me that a life well used is one that creates a beautiful space for others to dwell.

About the Author

Jeff Bowersox, author of *Finding Bishop Castle*, and wife Tammy, split time between their mountain home in Colorado and the Dominican Republic.

After a debilitating bout of Alcohol Use Disorder, Jeff has been sober since December 5th, 2016. Jeff and Tammy are committed to helping others take hold of the life of freedom and vibrancy that awaits them in recovery.

Jeff and Tammy operate Afterglow Escapes LLC, a venture dedicated to helping people in recovery experience sober beach vacations. They help maximize fun while mitigating the triggers that might lead to relapse.

Engage with our private Facebook community at https://www.facebook.com/groups/afterglowrecovery or for more information visit us at OurAfterglow.com.

Manufactured by Amazon.ca
Bolton, ON

22304170R00125